T5-AWI-067

DICE THROWN

PRINCETON ARCHITECTURAL PRESS

Dice Thrown

Benjamin Gianni

Bryan Shiles

Kevin Kemner

with an introduction by
Elysabeth Yates-Burns

Princeton Architectural Press

This catalogue has been made possible by the generous support of the Graham Foundation for Advanced Studies in the Fine Arts.

Thanks to Annetta Massey at Ohio State University and Dolores Gall at Yale Univ sity for helping to organize and facilitate the exhibitions of this work at the Unive sity Gallery at Ohio State and the Arts and Architecture Gallery at Yale. Thanks a to Mark Robbins, Sarah Willmer, and the members of Praxis for their support in t preparation of this work. Special thanks to Robert Livesey and the Department of Architecture at Ohio State University without whose support and encouragement this work would not be possible.

Published by
Princeton Architectural Press
37 East 7th Street
New York, New York 10003
212.995.9620

92 91 90 89 4 3 2 1

Production Editor: Elizabeth Short
Special thanks to Sheila Cohen, Clare Jacobson, Kevin Lippert,
Ann Urban, and Amy Weisser

Photo Credits:
Images on page 16 from Cornelius van de Ven, *Space in Architecture*
Plans on page 14 and 15 from John Reps, *Town Planning in Frontier America*

ISBN 0-910413-62-2

Gianni, Benjamin, 1958–
Dice thrown / Benjamin Gianni, Bryan Shiles, Kevin Kemner; with an introduc tion by Elysabeth Yates-Burns.
p. cm.
"The work contained in this catalogue has been exhibited at the following galleries: the University Gallery, Ohio State University, Columbus, Ohio, February 29 March 11, 1988; the Arts and Architecture Gallery, Yale University, New Haven, C necticut, October 24–November 4, 1988"—T.p. verso.
ISBN 0-910413-62-2 : $9.95
1. Farm buildings—United States—Themes, motives—Exhibitions. 2. Vernacul architecture—United States—Themes, motives—Exhibitions. 3. Architecture, Modern—20th Century—Europe—Themes, motives—Exhibitions. 4. Architecture Europe—Themes, motives—Exhibitions. Functionalism (Architecture)—Influence Exhibitions. 6. Enlightenment—Influence—Exhibitions.
I. Shiles, Bryan, 1959– . II. Kemner, Kevin, 1959– . III. Ohio State University. G lery of Fine Art. IV. Yale University. Art and Architecture Gallery. V. Title.
NA8201.G47 1989
728'.92'09730747468—dc20 89–33415
CIP

Table of Contents

Dice thrown will annull chance.

—Stéphane Mallarmé

God does not play games with dice.

—Albert Einstein

sabeth Yates-Burns

Search for a Method

erally, arguments that reference or
ak of the Modern abstractly or specifi-
y, i.e. in terms of modern literature,
lern philosophy, or modern architec-
, stress certain factors while disregard-
other equally significant and potential-
nlightening [though often contradic-
] points of view. For the most part,
which proposes a definitive outline of
it constitutes the Modern professes a
sparent argument. This is not a quali-
tion for the essay contained herein but
bservation of my own inability to
slate a definitive thesis. In fact, the
iction or subordination of knowledge
understanding to a set of systemic
racts does represent a prevalent thesis
Modernity. It is for this reason that I
e entitled the piece "Search for a
hod." After repeated attempts, I still
not lay claim to a sufficiently abso-
prolegomenon. In the end, perhaps, it
ne strength of my arguments that deny
operly hierarchical definition.

A Klee painting named "Angelus Novus" shows an angel looking as though he is about to move away from something he is fixedly contemplating. His eyes are staring, his mouth is open, his wings are spread. This is how one pictures the angel of history. His face is turned toward the past. Where we perceive a chain of events, he sees one single catastrophe which keeps piling wreckage upon wreckage and hurls it in front of his feet. The angel would like to stay, awaken the dead, and make whole what has been smashed. But a storm is blowing from Paradise; it has got caught in his wings with such violence that the angel can no longer close them. This storm irresistibly propels him into the future to which his back is turned, while the pile of debris before him grows skyward. This storm is what we call progress.

Walter Benjamin, *Illuminations*

During the winter and spring of 1987, I had the opportunity to work and conduct research in West Berlin. The research work was to be on the theories of time and space [late nineteenth- and early twentieth-century science] and their consequent impact on the development of pedagogical methodology and the work of students and faculty at the Bauhaus in Weimar and Dessau. Of special interest to me was the work of Paul Klee, in particular his Vorkurs and Nature Study courses. The research was to culminate in a study entitled, albeit with reservations, "Vergil/Beatrice" or "Reason and Intuition." Naturally, as is the case with many well intended research projects, my plans were changed—not immediately, but as a matter of course—to include the particularities of the city of Berlin, the presence of which I have never been able to articulate adequately. I had carried a copy of Benjamin's quote with me in hopes of locating those particular support sketches or notes, which I, in fact, did. As might be expected, the passage became something more significant with each passing day. Walking the streets of this perpetually estranged city, it occurred to me that its aged residue, so thick on the facades and rubble of a defeated and celebrated architecture, seemed to live as much in the hidden cracks of the stone walks as it did in the faces of the Berliners. It is unimaginable to me what the city and its people have known in the five hundred years since the city's inception. In becoming engaged with Berlin, it seemed that there was only one problem that needed to be addressed, and that was history. It is currently inconceivable to me how architects and historians of architecture can be content with the leavings of so many stylistic permutations of names, dates, numbers, and so on. History itself, in the very real architectural sense, is something at once both more concrete and more ineffable. Standing near the Berlin Wall, looking in one direction down the Strasse de 17 Juni as it splits the Tiergarten, and then in the other direction through the Brandenburg

Gate, past the Reichstag, and then farther to East Berlin's "Mainstrasse" Unter den Linden, it occurred to me that the Wall was that which represented history as both its facticity and its ineffableness; it was there that I first understood the significanc of architecture as that which exists through, by, and of history, as history exists through, by, and of architecture. The Wall itself, a feat of the nineteenth and twentieth centuries' Sisyphean struggle with history, is seemingly inevitable and irrevocable, as of a latent condition, while at the same time suggesting—even revealing—its temporariness given the immediacy of its response and the absurdity of it proposition. Yet still, it is that marker, that trace of history—a literal presence of th absence—that none of us can either deny or confront. In essence, it is the capable use of the interrogative as an imperative.

I suggested this metaphor to a colleague of mine recently. Despite a tepid reacti at first, he soon pondered the problem, agreeing that history—or rather the crisis o paradox of history as I have referred to it in the past—is that which characterizes and possesses Modern architecture. Clearly, it is not a stylistic or phenomenal appropriation but an ideological one. Given a readership most often bent on formalis and aesthetics, I do not expect that such an assertion will be acceptable. Even to myself, history is no longer all-inclusive when discussing the shape of Modernity. My original intention for study—the theories of time and space—piqued my consciousness again and again, at which point it was suggested by yet another colleag that we might suppose science as yet another preeminent task of Modernity. In fac I am completely willing to accept this proposition, but only to add yet a third con tion that has also surfaced repeatedly, and that is the question of being and existence, commonly referred to as the ontological.

More recently, I came across some work of Anselm Kiefer, whom I had seen re resented in Berlin, in Chicago. The problem of architecture and history, particular in the "Shulamite," "Athanor," and "Dem unbekannten Maler [To an Unknown Painter]," surfaces yet again. In asserting that history is transcribed as a text in bui form, I am told that I have entered into a neo-Gothic phase in my work. Though w ing to accept this, it is purely on account of having seen Wim Wender's recent film "Wings of Desire," in which angels occupy the city of Berlin. The Wall, story-telli and history are all prominent themes, as is the city of Berlin itself. It seemed that of the pieces were in place.

When asked to write something for the exhibition that accompanies this catalogue, I was intrigued by its proposal, especially as it is represented vis-a-vis the author's essay, "American Vernacular: A Prototype for Modernism." I, of course, s about trying to determine the hidden clauses in the statement, last of all unearthing—as is usually the case—the possibility of stylistic or formalistic connotations. They seem trivial at this point. The real issue, should there be one, is, as suggeste above, that of the "Modern." I do believe that somewhere in the studies of science history, and ontology [being and existence] are the clues for such an exposé. I am proposing this trio of conditions—science, history, and the ontic—as that which most fully describes or delimits Modernity, and particularly that which is specific a thesis on Modern architecture. Through this we might ascertain the coincidents that suggest an American vernacular. Though everything works against it, I believ along with Klee, Benjamin, Wenders, Kiefer, and Beuys, that we ultimately are ab to ascertain the associations necessary to form a distinct impression, however fleeting or remote. Still, it is the angels who know the real story.

As a modern problem, the first condition, history, is touched on above, albeit from a poetic—even phenomenological—point of view. There are a few additional observations that might be made. Certainly, the centrality of history has played a role in formulating the codification of both the vernacular and the Modern. In confronting the problem of history, the vernacular does not suggest a notion of progress, but rather the a-temporal valuation of tradition. Likewise, it might also be asserted that Modern, despite some rhetoric to the contrary, sought an architecture that refrained from suggesting contemporaneity. Modernist rhetoric prescribed an architecture that existed after the end of historical time, professing a point of view consistent with Hegel's pronouncements of a kind of universal dominion at and after the end of history and the death of art. What was supposed was a kind of absolute architecture, dependent only on its autonomous identity. This was, of course, one of the internal contradictions in some Modernist rhetoric, i.e. how to be "new," [which implies an "old" and a "con-temporaneity"], yet still be entirely present. Moreover, the death of art, which includes by implication architecture, supposes an end to dissension. It is unclear whether such a protest must continue ad infinitum, or if a nirvana—at the end to rebellion—will result from the absolute nature of an unmediated and redoubtable architecture of consensus.

Our second condition, science, is perhaps the most generalized and abstracted of the three. History and ontology depend on science as an epistemological construct. In the world as we know it, science has significantly informed, if not founded, our understanding of both the abstract and the concrete nature of our modern existence.

One of the more significant developments in modern mathematics is the discovery or, depending on your point of view, invention of non-Euclidean geometry. According to Euclidean geometry, we live in a world of perfect, absolute geometrical structures which are extensions of pure mind. The point, line, plane, and solid volumes of Euclidean geometry are that which we "know" versus that which we "experience." Non-Euclidean geometry is closer to our experience. It is a world where there can be a number of straight lines that meet at one point, thereby enclosing an area (the lines of latitude, parallel at the equator and culminating in a single point at the North and South Poles is a simple illustration of non-Euclidean geometry.) Because the earth curves and because our experience is part of this world-view, so do parallel lines converge at either end. Obviously, it depends on which geometry or "system" you choose to employ when discussing the truth of a given proposition. In the end, it is both "experience" and "knowing" that constitute the summation of understanding. One cannot be considered more correct than another. Moreover, the context, or system itself, determines the truth or falsehood of a given resolution or goal with respect to its hypothesis. This is what is oft-times referred to as scientific or vertical thinking.

I would like to suggest that the site of the Modern exists in both a non-Euclidean and Euclidean universe, one that is described most aptly as the resolution of two distinct sets of site conditions. In this particular case, it is as though the site of the vernacular occupies a given plane, while the Modern occupies yet another. Both equations exist in space and time simultaneously, though their reference is quite different. Ultimately, the relationship between these two site conditions is essentially non-Euclidean, as that of two non-parallel, non-intersecting planes. There are proximate relationships, even potential relationships, but the summation, given th foreclosed system and origin of either, particularly with respect to one another, is cidental and imaginary. Though we also operate in a Euclidean universe, that universe implies a consequent summation. I caution that we may not, even should not, describe a single point of view when the systems and methods that define it a essentially isolated. It is only the method or system, by definition internalized, tha operates critically; either set of conditions are entirely local, and again [as referred to previously as scientific thinking] by definition, isolated.

As an effective critique of methodology and systemics, no twentieth-century art work has expressed this point with as much impact as Marcel Duchamp's ironic "Bride Stripped Bare By Her Bachelors Even" or "Large Glass." A methodical and entirely hermetic narrative, the piece portends to suggest, perhaps define, that which is method vis-a-vis the appearance of a system or method. Duchamp, as do Mallarmé [who will be discussed below], suggests that classification, a primary co ponent of scientific thinking, of linguistic and visual concepts, is essentially formu lated around the arbitrary. In a commentary on method as representation, convention is no longer considered to be absolute; Duchamp unravels the consciousness the without of "technique" in recording the very thin threshold of an ever-transmu table meaning from within. The immeasurable is the primary captive of our own i agination—the inexplicable, unmediated freedoms we assume are only too soon codified, lapsing into a swell of disuse. But such is the tendency of the abstract ov the concrete. As in the "Large Glass," it is our imagination that allows us discours yet it is freedom that facilitates order.

Alain Robbe-Grillet's thesis in *For a New Novel* articulates a similar concern. In critique of the pre-eminent nature of systemization and methodology, he conclude

Now that the world is neither meaningful nor absurd, it simply is... in place of the universe of "meanings" [psychological, social, functional] one should try to construc more solid, more immediate world. So that first of all it will be through their presenc that objects and gestures will impose themselves, and so that this presence continues thereafter to dominate, beyond any theory of explication that might attempt to enclo them in any sort of sentimental, sociological, Freudian, metaphysical, or any other sy tem of reference.

Both Robbe-Grillet and Duchamp contend that given the descriptive nature of science as a fundamental bias, traditional operatives, i.e. metaphor—whether humanis ideological, or historical—no longer motivate. It is implied that what were qualitative positions are displaced by quantitative criteria; "meaning" is conditioned by function, utility, method, and systemics. The complicity of the abstract notions of "structure," "use," "site-specificity," "materials," "construction," and "systems" is that which dete mines the "function" of the building as architecture. The program, as per the tradition mediators of the history and language of architecture, is presented as a tabula rasa. Th potential for a reductio ad absurdum [re: Duchamp's Green Book] is obvious, particula ly in terms of the contention of a self-evident reason and necessity. Yet again, how could the contention of reason and necessity express conditional criteria, especially that which is architectural?

There is only one problem... the one posed by the non-necessitous nature of language. Owing to language, human energy does not seem to be entirely transmitted in the course of its transformations... There is too much play in the gears. [Parain]

Uncertainty beggars silence. How does one make use of something that is no longer absolute? The Modern language of architecture stood for, though it did not activate, a kind of autonomy. In disregarding history as a motive, the search for a language of architecture became a degree-zero proposition—a meaning condition beyond metaphor, that, by implication, suggests the fictive, groundless [and self-evident] nature of historicist thinking. As with Heisenberg's polemical assertion of the discontinuous nature of quantum physics—contrary to Einstein's position—so too does Modern architecture represent the gamble of an attempt at formulating a thesis at a zero degree. History may no longer indicate or instill value; its replacement is the abstract and seemingly absolute, yet conditional, method of science. In choosing science as Modern architecture's muse, the difficulties of presuming the descriptive nature of science arise. In the search for a language of architecture, science is seen, on the one hand, as both a traditional means of representation and, on the other, as that which informs method. In the struggle for meaning in architecture, both method and metaphor are transposed, even as method and metaphor, as operatives, are essentially contraposed. In light of this, we have Modern intentions in architecture that are simultaneously driven by a concern for method or process as the instigator of truth and meaning, and product, or the thing in itself, as the bearer of meaning. At once, the object is synchronically preeminent and anesthetized.

Consequently, one might ask is it the means or the ends with which we concern ourselves—or both? As mentioned previously, the systems that underlie either intention [method versus traditional meaning, or simply process versus product] are inherently contraposed. Similarly, what is the criteria for evaluation that takes precedent? As in Heisenberg's explanation of the uncertainty principle, the criteria, the instruments for measuring, can never be internally or externally absolute. In Modern architecture, the tendency of both an internally absolute [descriptive] and an in-absolute [metaphoric] criteria exist [and at times exchange places], though they are obviously contradictory measures. Moreover, there is a separation between a criterion that harbors a regard for the "what" of meaning, versus that which speaks to the "how" or "why" of meaning.

In searching for the "how" or "why" of the vernacular, in light of our so-called Modern architecture, it can be asserted that it is the landscape that motivates. Whether it is the horizontality of Wright's mediation between earth and sky, or the skyscraper, that parable of reason and necessity and the supreme circumstance of the individual that characterizes our cities, the architecture, as ourselves, exists in an unparalleled wealth. Yet still we confront a similar problem as that which has been addressed above. Is it the abstract landscape, the degree zero, that we ascertain as it is presented in the associated material? Is it merely the ever-deferring horizon that conditions our viewpoint? I am told that many of those involved in the westward expansion of this country actually engaged an "infinitude" whereupon the sense of one's individuated self becomes manifest, as an aporiatic and existential freedom which, in the end, amounts to knowing neither from whence they came to where they were going. In the abstraction of this country's mapping, via the in tive and non-hierarchical Cartesian grid of Jefferson's plan, one cannot fail to note peculiar lack of place, as though it had little relevance [much as it is expressed herein]. It is as if location itself were merely a descriptive, quantitative condition, and that place, the requisite of the specific and the particular of any location, did not exist. Is there a set of events that signifies both simultaneously? It is quite dif- ficult to imagine the coincidence of the descriptive term location and the meta- phoric explanation of place. Such an outline is conditioned by two very different sets of parameters. Again, the systems are not interchangeable but potentially con tradictory, yet we suspend doubt in recognizing the validity of both.

What was it that Sartre illustrated in "John Dos Passos" and "1919" or "Ameri Cities?" In a collection that also contains "Departure and Return," "Cartesian Free dom" and "Materialism and Revolution," was there a general narrative implied? Given the vernacular landscape, I am reminded of his dogmatic and unconditiona "authenticity," that absolute degree of unimpeded self as pronounced by the su- preme existentialist virtue of "good faith." The narrative itself, understood as it is the individual, is forever becoming, yet its conditional authenticity is absolute. T objective is inescapably modern, the proto-rational signifying the ironic self-conta ment of autonomy. It is not that this autonomy is irrespective of others, but rather that it does not exist for others. It denies the possibility of an other's responsibilit and it does not allow for "bad faith," or self-deception. But, as Sartre himself im- plored while first visiting America: what of the conformism of individualism? Yet again, the accompanying work expresses the complicit tendency of both measures

In grappling with an eventually nihilistic tendency of existentialism in the lan scape of the Modern mind, the sculptor and painter Giacommetti designed the ico nic Joshua tree of Beckett's "Godot." Nothing more could add to the irreverent humor that Beckett describes. In the California desert, there exists the metaphor f such an individual, Sartre's player also, one who knows nothing of the joy of tran sience, but only the inevitability of such. It is the same alienated and singular lan scape as that of Cartesian space we see represented herein, that unmediated remo of difference and, more importantly, of end. It is as though we, as is that which su rounds us, are always and only self-evident in terms of reason and necessity, facin few, if any, parameters. There is not a word to describe it aptly, merely dimension tending towards an insistent and compliant doubt. Should we then speak instead, Nietzsche, of the annihilation of language? There is something akin to Beckett's *Texts for Nothing* in Molly's Monologue—muses underlining the inevitability and necessity of a Siren's Song, no matter the end of language. As wordlessness con- gregates, the ontological and epistemological exchange places—though perhaps, in complying with pure method, it is really that they become transparent to each oth

In the accompanying work that this catalogue represents, the appropriation of Mallarmé's poetry recalls Sartre's transfigurative "bad faith" or self-deception. The inherent contradictions that suggest the bad faith of Modern architecture are, for t most part, simply rhetorical and, therefore, do not inform the "site" of vernacular chitecture. As was suggested earlier, it might be that there are coincidents. Some these are outlined quite clearly, while others are only alluded to. It is troublesome that such happenstance might be reduced to mere formalism. Even in the loosely held layout of these observations, there are a significant number of relationships, some that reach beyond pure rhetoric, while some might actually be regarded as "causal." One of the least important issues—even trivial at first glance—is the thesis title, "Dice Thrown." Stéphane Mallarmé's poem, "Dice Thrown Twice Will Annul Chance," expresses the impossibility of the arbitrary in a world where the existence of any two establishes a relationship, portending a totality or even closure. Such are the clever words of Einstein's critique of Heisenberg's positions; "God does not play dice." This simple nature of duality itself, that which is one thing and then another simultaneously, expressly implies association, even if based only on proximity. The formation of a narrative is recognized immediately, though its contention, ironically unlike much of modernist rhetoric, is never absolute. It is not only a world in which the arbitrary cannot not exist—it is a world in which the arbitrary, chance itself, is unrecognizable.

In entering into a discourse on the idea of the Modern, I am always confronted immediately with disparity. I am particularly amused by the seeming self-abnegation of the notion of experience in Modern architecture, particularly as it is beclouded by the rhetorical. It seems impossible to regard "an experience of the abstract," "the rhetorical," or "the methodical." Yet this is, ironically in this case, what we have in much of a so-called vernacular farm architecture. It is the experience of the abstract that purveys such poetry—vis-a-vis the romantic simplicity or "honesty" of the buildings themselves, begotten by an unselfconscious and unmediated reason and necessity. Its presumption of an abstract site is entirely real—all that must exist for what it is, no more, no less. The only real context is something as simultaneously concrete and ineffable as the Berlin Wall—the horizon. I am not in any way suggesting that it was such a set of criteria that begat Modern architecture, though some parallels may exist. In both cases, the abstract is made concrete; yet in the vernacular there is the suspension of all doubt, whereas in the Modern dictum the motivation is doubt. Neither demeans the other, but I have yet to ascertain the equation that effectively affords summation, or an integration between them. I may only return to my earlier metaphor, founded in the research of a site. There indeed exist two non-parallel, non-intersecting conditions that are proximate, though their absolute association is unfounded and inconsistent. Such closure becomes mere rhetoric—which neither founds nor promotes architecture.

njamin Gianni

American Farm Vernacular: A Prototype For Modernism?

v between houses. Mackinack Island, Michigan

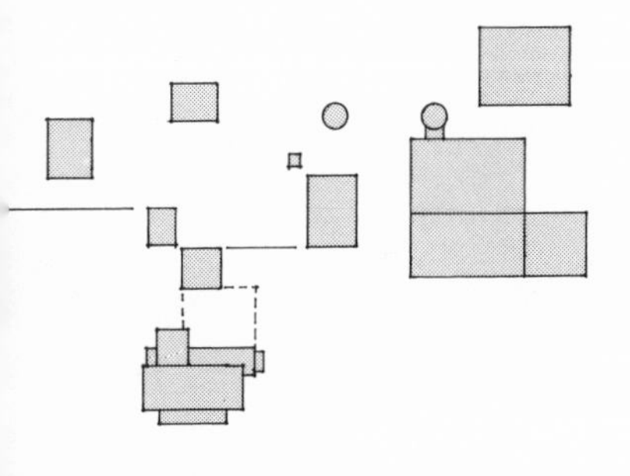

ı of farm 4. Central Ohio

In the late 19th century a group of farmers emigrated from a village in Germany to a region of southern Ohio—among them was the grandfather of a colleague of mine. Together they purchased a six-square-mile parcel of land and subdivided it into individual farms. Remembering the open landscapes of southern Ohio and individual farmsteads which crowned disparate knolls, my friend was surprised to find, upon visiting his ancestral village, that it was organized in a completely different way. The German farmsteads were grouped together to form a collectivity, outside of and around which lay the fields.

Upon returning from Germany the question was asked: having bought the land in Ohio together, why did you not organize it like the village you left? His grandfather pondered a moment and answered: I don't know. It just wasn't done that way here.

In architectural theory it is often suggested that the salient differences between American and European city form are due to the plays of self-interest which have influenced the development of the American city. In this scenario the typological obscurity of the American city is related to the phenomenon of late capitalism—the implicit suggestion being that if one or another interest were to predominate, city form would be more cohesive. While this seems reasonable, it is interesting to measure this argument against the typology of the farm compound, where, under the jurisdiction of a single owner, similar extra-formal relationships predominate. This prompts us to re-evaluate the form of the American city in relation to the form of the farmstead, analyzing them in tandem and according to their own aspirations rather than in relation to European urban precedents. We must re-examine the preconception that the American city aspires to the spatial and formal morphology of the European city.

Furthermore, given the agrarian underpinnings of American society, it is impossible to separate the morphology of the farm compound from the morphology of the city. The two are historically allied and, as in the example above, directly determine one another.

The American farm compound is organized in a manner radically different from its European counterpart. While the European farmstead is predominantly a closed compound organized around a courtyard, the American farm is comprised of disparate and individuated buildings whose integration around a definable farmyard is loose at best. In all of my research on American farm complexes I have never come

View of farm 6. Central Ohio

Shaker structure. Shakertown, Kentucky

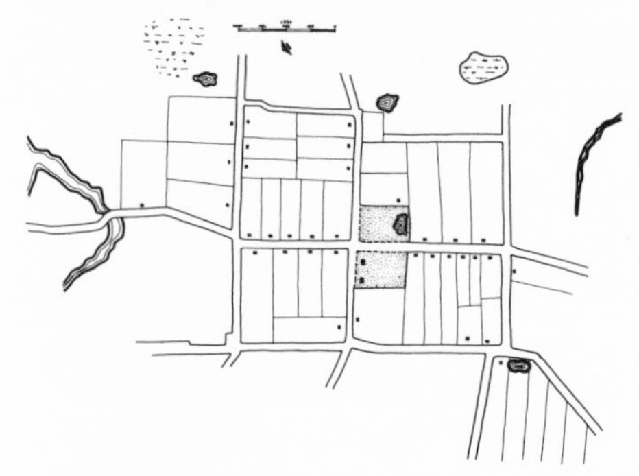

Plan of Fairfield Connecticut, 1640

across a description, visual or verbal, of the farm compound as a whole. Even in farmer's guides and how-to literature, the farm is always presented as a collection distinct objects. While comparable English texts suggest the grouping of farm func tions around a common courtyard, the notion of a definable court is virtually unknown in American farm planning. Space is never figural nor closed—buildings remain autonomous and their autonomy is neither questioned nor compromised b the possibility of an organizational spatial figure. Beyond functional exigency, farn organization, as such, is never mentioned.

Finally, it is interesting to suggest that, in its avoidance of formally aligned and axially resolved composition, the farmstead is more closely aligned with the principles of Modernism (as they manifested themselves in European architecture in t early part of this century) than with any given precedent. Both architectures reject resolution for spatially open-ended arrangements of form; both prefer dynamic co position to the stasis of symbolic geometry; the structural conditions of both allow the facade or elevation to be posited on wholly new terms, playing upon the compositional potentials of a non-loadbearing skin.

As a comparative analysis of city form to farm compound configuration can off new insights into the forces which motivate urban form, so too can a comparative analysis of rural vernacular building to early Modernist architecture suggest genealogical connections which might broaden our understanding of both.

Background

It is helpful to set the stage by examining certain predispositions latent in early American architecture—namely, the use of the freestanding building ("object") an an open attitude to the landscape.

1. Given that the earliest settlers were English, it bears mentioning that English architecture has been traditionally more disposed toward the pavilion (freestanding structure) than continental European architecture. Climatic conditions made the courtyard type less favorable in England, and, more importantly, being circumscribed by water, England was less vulnerable to attack. The lack of a strong need for fortifications led to a tradition of freestanding buildings in landscapes mc open than one finds elsewhere.

2. The development of most European towns can be traced to the feudal period during which a merchant class was forming. These towns evolved as service-base entities most often within the confines of fortifications. In this tradition a strong physical, cultural, and economic distinction was made between the city and the s rounding countryside; farmers lived outside the city and interacted with it only at designated points and times.

By contrast, the vast majority of American cities were founded as essentially agrarian ventures. As such, neither a formal nor economic dichotomy existed between the city and the country. Not only did the absence of fortifications allow fo much looser fabric of buildings and open views through the city to the landscape beyond, but a piece of the surrounding landscape was often brought into the cente of town as a Common or grazing pasture. In a fundamental way the distinction be-

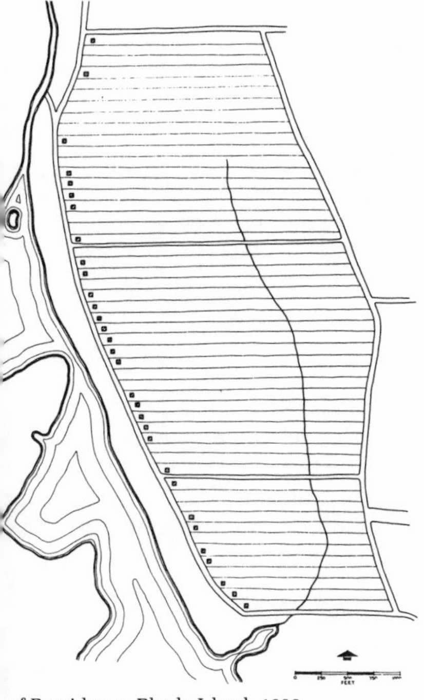
of Providence, Rhode Island, 1638

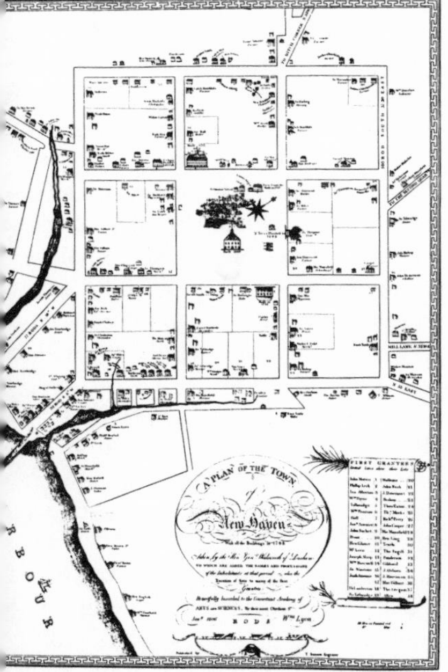
of New Haven, Connecticut, 1748

tween city and landscape was blurred. Through the loose grouping of buildings, open-ended street patterns, and incorporation of pasturelands, the concept of inside and outside was not only de-emphasized but intentionally subverted. Wilderness formed both the boundary and the center of the city.

3. Both urban and regional decentralization further diffused the formal hierarchy of American towns. As essentially communistic ventures, Pilgrim settlements avoided strong formal and civic hierarchy in their town plans. The predominant organizational device of the grid, while having a long history in town planning, took on new meaning in the context of these democratic societies. Being unbounded by fortifications (unlike Greek and Roman precedents), the grid-iron lost a clearly defined center. And where formally suggested, as in the nine-square cities of New England, the potentially hierarchical reading of the center was diffused by its use as pastureland.

A like attitude of decentralization characterized the regional settlement patterns of New England. Following the example of the Early Church, the size of communities was monitored, and new communities were formed when a given parent community had reached its limit. As such, the hierarchical, "all-roads-lead" phenomenon of a given capital city was avoided; power and population remained diffuse. In the structure of their governments and towns the colonies were seen as autonomous and interconnected units forming a network across the countryside. Towns remained open to the landscape and cognizant of the communities beyond them.

GENEALOGY #1: COMMON HERITAGE IN THE EIGHTEENTH CENTURY

Given that the above tendencies existed before the colonies began to coalesce in the 18th Century, it is interesting to note the strong similarity of early town plans and settlement patterns to the ideals which came to characterize the culture of the Enlightenment. Within the context of this observation one can argue the sensibilities of the Enlightenment as fundamental to cultural and architectural Modernism.

The Enlightenment and the "idea" of America were not only contemporaneous but also shared a common ideological grounding in the myth of Arcadia. Resisting the Church's doctrine of Original Sin, the Arcadian myth held that man had once dwelled upon the earth in a state of perfection. As such, evil was not the inevitable consequence of a fallen human nature, but the overlap of self-interest in a poorly organized society. Arcadia formed the basis of a revisionist history which put perfection back within the grasp of human nature. Positing that man had once lived in a perfect "State of Nature," it became reasonable that mankind might again achieve perfection. Religious rebirth gave way to social and political reorganization.

This revision carried important consequences for the conception of architectural form and its relation to the physical world. Within both the Christian and Greek schemas, nature, being "once-removed" from perfection, could at best allude to ideals in a representational way. As such architectural form was essentially symbolic—both a geometric distillation of the physical world and an image of the heavens. Like man himself, architecture occupied a middle ground between the chaos of nature and the perfection of divinity. It was an artificial world in which

Peaceable Kingdom Edward Hicks

Funeral of Phocion Nicholas Poussin, 1648

space and form were manipulated to align with the heavenly world beyond. Architecture opposed nature in the direction of its aspirations.

With the Arcadian myth came a re-evaluation both of nature and of the essenti ly representational function of architecture. If nature were perfect apart from the deleterious effects of human intervention, architecture might well aspire to Natur substituting natural and nostalgic allusion for conceptual and/or geometric manipulation as its *modus operandi*. The operative set of references would no longer be vertical (heavenward) but lateral (historical and natural); architecture could confront the world around it, not for what might be latent in it or distilled from it, but as it was. In so doing, architecture could open itself up to the idea of landscape. Leaving symbolism to the architectural object, space could fracture its geometric frame of reference and re-evaluate its symbolic grounding in light of an idealized vision of the wilderness.

The idea of "starting over" and the discovery of the New World went hand in hand. While certainly the political philosophy of the Enlightenment led to serious challenges to the hierarchical organization of European society, it was the overwhelming experience of the revolutionaries that the time-bound culture of Europe resisted change. One need only confront the irony of the coronation of Napoleon the outcome of the French Revolution to understand the extent of this resistance. Grounded as it was in the hierarchy of Greco-Christian thought, society sought to concentrate power and cleave to an image of the absolute. Only within the contex of a New World could a new society be effectively formed.

In this context America played the double role of an unspoilt Arcadia and the ting for a new political Utopia. Grounded in the belief in an Arcadia, the Utopian visions of a "Paradise Regained" motivated the sensibilities of the Enlightenment, mingling freely with visions of a New Jerusalem already present in the Pilgrim se sibility. Images such as Edward Hicks's "Peaceable Kingdom" demonstrate the extent to which political and religious visions of America were elided.

With the suspicious rejection of political hierarchy came an implicit rejection formal hierarchy in the organization of the physical world. The democratic overtones of a new society brought with them an implicit demand for a new organizational system. Present in this was the embracing of the purified idea of wilderness as a viable alternative to urbanity. To integrate with nature was to remain both linked to original perfection and to anticipate the day when the lion would again lay down with the lamb. The implications of wilderness as the formal prototype f urban organization, however, necessitated a new definition of urbanity, for wilderness and urbanity had been traditionally opposed. Loosely, then, it was a fragmented landscape of individual buildings which supplanted the image of the den and inwardly focused cities of Europe. The cities of the New World would eviden a reticence to manipulate the physical environment; they would be reticent to manipulate space, as Paradise was no longer gained artificially by reference to sy bolic geometries but by integration with Nature itself.

It bears acknowledging that these revisions in political and organizational idea made reference to 18th century science. Both the Arcadian myth and the notion o the perfection of Nature draw directly upon the work of Sir Isaac Newton, whose laws of thermodynamics and motion demonstrated that physical matter operated

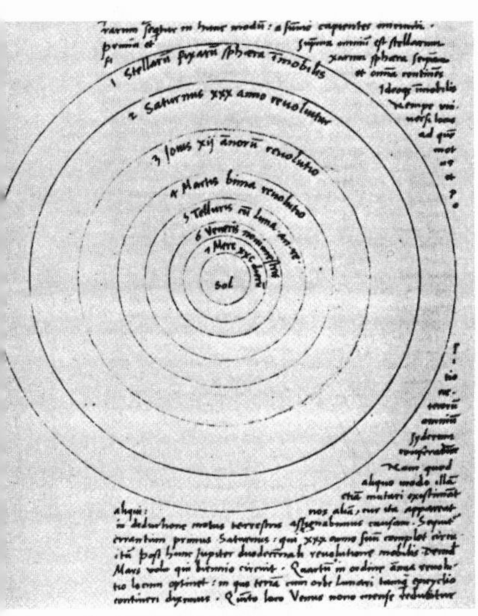

rnican diagram of universe

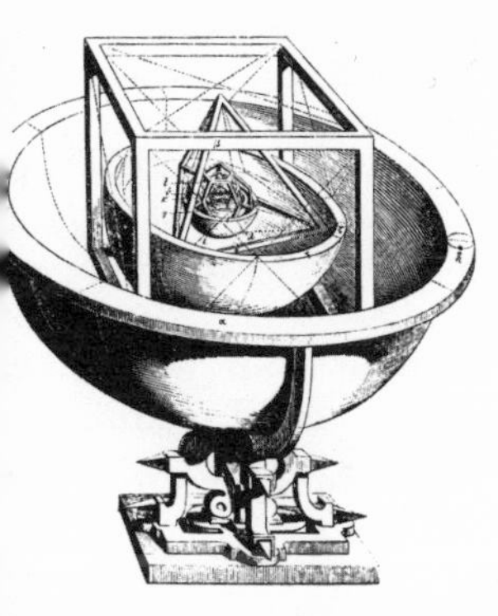

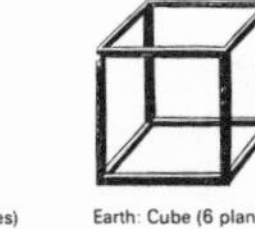

nnes Kepler, diagram of cosmological structure

perfect and consistent ways. As with the displacement of Paradise from the heavenly realm to the spatio-temporal (historical) realm of Arcadia, Newton's work implied a "handing down" of perfection from the ideal or conceptual realm to the physical world at hand. Divinity was displaced into space and time—it was now a property of the physical.

As in Enlightenment philosophy, these "discoveries" prompted the re-evaluation of nature. Like human nature, it no longer appeared base and representationally linked to perfection, but demonstratively perfect in its workings. The conception of nature as a chaos from which one might abstract geometric truth was challenged by those who would deify Nature itself. The traditional role of the architect as geometric necromancer had to be revised.

While the implications of this are far reaching in the history of architecture, fundamental among them is the change in the status of space. Building upon Descartes' redefinition of space as "res extensia," Newton's concept of Absolute Space described the universe as infinite in extension. While supporting geometric calibration, space defied geometric definition—breaking free of the parameters of the perfect sphere in which Aristotle had inscribed it and in which it had remained until the 18th century. The traditional alliance of space, geometry, and architecture was severed. The nested geometries of the Baroque, so close to Kepler's diagrams of the universe, gave way to a radically neutral and non-directional field. As such, the representation of space in Enlightened architecture was problematic. No longer an identifiable thing in and of itself, space now functioned as the great ground on which the objects of the world were read. It was the absolute difference between things; the difference between observer and observed. Cartesian space functioned as a three-dimensional matrix in which the objects of the world could be organized. It was simultaneously the presumption and the possibility of objectivity; the projection of the infinite space of the mind onto the physical world. It was the possibility of identification which was, in turn, the prerequisite for objective manipulation and the groundwork both for science and for the concept of progress. Having been geometrically neutralized, the notion of "space" was dissociated from the traditionally bounded and definable notion of "place." Form alone was left to carry meaning.

While this "extensive" conception of space can be demonstrated in myriad examples of European architecture (from the floating dome of Wren's St. Stephen's Walbrook to the freestanding and sequentially ordered pavilions of the English garden), the overwhelming presence of the urban context in Europe kept manifestations isolated and incidental. Within the city the freestanding building remained an essentially theoretical proposition.

Rather, it was in the planning of America that these spatial ideals came to fruition. In its reaction to the hierarchies of European society, America functioned as both a genesis and a repository for the ideals of the Enlightenment. In this context it is reasonable that it should be upon the North American continent that "atopia" (placelessness) would be realized.

Aerial view of Kansas showing continental grid

House by a Railroad Edward Hopper 1925

Shaker structure. Shakertown, Kentucky

The Role of Thomas Jefferson

We have noted that much of early American planning anticipated the principles which came to characterize the Enlightenment: i.e., lack of formalized relationshi open spatial connections with the landscape, integration of "wilderness" with urbanity in the form of a town green, few formalized spaces, rejection of hierarchy, etc., as well as the democratic overtones and utopian visions of the American religious and political milieu. In this context, the role of Jefferson, as the primary player in the transmission of Enlightenment ideals to the planning of America, wa to extend what was already in place on the level of the community to the scale of the country as a whole. This was accomplished by means of the continental grid— the system of six-square-mile township divisions which were laid over the territories west of the Alleghenies in 1789.

Beyond the functional expedience of the grid as a surveying tool, the use of the grid was motivated by an explicit desire to effect decentralization. It was the form manifestation of Jefferson's unequivocally anti-urban sentiments. In clear rejection the urban-centered society of Europe, Jefferson planned the North American continent as an equal network of townships, each with its own local government, schools, and common lands. Like the Pilgrim settlements before them, these communities were conceived as autonomous but interconnected agrarian units.

The extensive planning of the continent, then, not only reflects the ideology of society suspicious of absolute government and the dis-economies of urban scale, b was effected by means of a formal device, the grid, which brought with it the "pla less" aspects of the Cartesian or Newtonian universe. Within the framework of the continental grid, townships were not situated in relation to favorable geographic c ditions (rivers, etc.) but were situated abstractly, as a consequence of calibrated su divisions. The position of a town was topographically arbitrary, falling every sixth square mile across the continent. The idea of *location* (as locus or microclimate) was formally superceded by the idea of *position* within a larger web of interstices. Never before in the history of town planning had a more poignant dissociation between position and place been made. (A similar disregard for place characterized th towns laid out by the railway companies in the 19th century. Towns were position along a given railway line based on the distance a farmer could travel to a depot an make it home by dark. Like a majority of the township towns, the survey of these towns preceded their buildings and inhabitants. Previously inaccessible lands were bought by the companies and sold to would-be farmers on the East Coast.)

Implicit, then, in the planning of Jefferson's township towns was not only this i cidental connection to topographic amenities, but also a loose infrastructure interwoven with commons and farmlands. Predominant within this scene was the frees tanding building, the icon of the spirit of individualism which formed the basis of the American collectivity. Institutionalizing the example of its Puritan predecesso the town in no way attempted to turn inward nor contain the highways which passed through it en route to other towns. The gridded town plan was understood as a subdivision of the larger continental grid to which it deferred; its spatial refer ences remained broad and non-specific. Both its position and plan tended toward the "atopic."

eau of *Marly* J.H. Mansard 1687

aving of University of Virginia, Charlottesville, By B. Tanner 1826

In this respect we also acknowledge an alliance between the city and the farmstead. The individuated buildings of the farmstead and their loose disposition at right angles within the gridded countryside parallel the disposition of structures within the town grid. Both the town and the farm forsake geometrically defined plazas and courtyards for spaces which operate on a much broader scale. In their open-endedness and in their respective grids both the city and the farm make reference to the organization of the continent.

Even the institutions of 18th century America reflect this morphological agenda. Looking at Jefferson's plan for the University of Virginia, for example, one sees a clear reference to the Chateau of Marly. Jefferson's transformations of this prototype, however, are symptomatic of the desire to further breakdown the spatial figurality which the forearms of Marly challenged. By differentiating the pavilions, Jefferson disrupted the repetitious continuity of the edges, asserting the figurality of the compositional elements over/against the space of the lawn which they enclose. In so doing he also makes reference to two pre-existent American types—the Main Street town and the Strip Farm town—both of which are comprised of individuated pavilions organized along a line. While differences remain, the spirit is similar.

From building to farmstead to town, then, we may observe a fundamental connection between the spatial and formal proclivities of American planning, and the transformations in architecture precipitated by Enlightenment thought. Jefferson's direct contact with France as ambassador during the time between the two revolutions is to some extent responsible, for architecture in 18th-century France was undergoing a transformation toward the pavilion. More importantly, the demotic underpinnings of American culture and the demise of the monarchy in France supported similar political and architectural sensibilities. These sensibilities were, in turn, reinforced by the sciences, whose grounding in empiricism (Cartesian method) reversed the direction of reasoning from downward to upward, rejecting the a priori assumption or given description of unity. The idea of empiricism supported the opinions and observations of the individual, dispersing the power to know among the common lot of man. Knowledge was not "received" from on high, but achieved through reason, observation, and use of the senses. The notion of knowledge had changed, moving away from questions of meaning to questioning the process itself.

It is within the context of empiricism that the idea of the vernacular—the people's architecture—gains ascendancy. It is an architecture whose condition of meaning works from the ground upward. It does not operate iconographically but functionally, economically, and efficaciously. As such, the vernacular is an empiricist architecture concerned more with the facilitating of process than with explicit questions of divine or cultural representation. It is an architecture of method (function) rather than meaning.

GENEALOGY #2: RIEGL, HEGEL AND HUGO

While it is beyond the scope of this essay to offer a comprehensive definition of architectural Modernism, it is helpful to look at its development in 19th century thought in relation to the ideas of the 19th century theorist Alois Riegl.

Pyramid of Menkaura, Giza

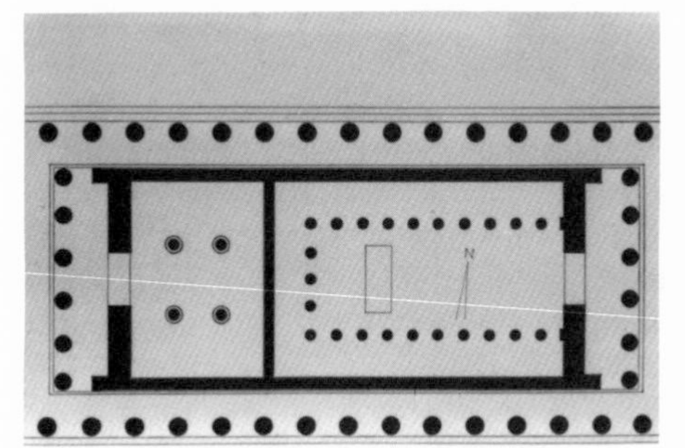

Plan of the Parthenon. Acropolis, Athens

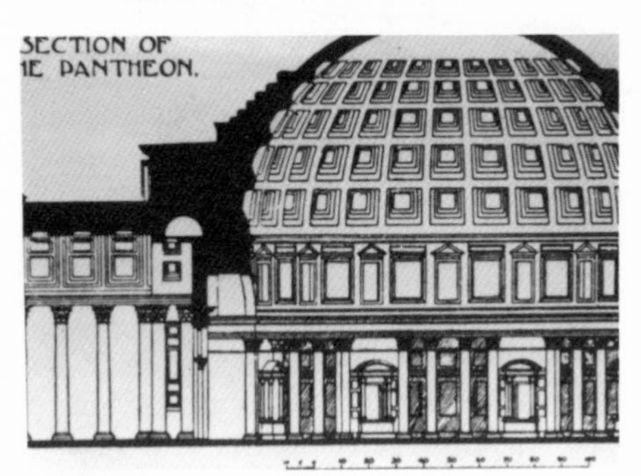

Longitudinal section. Pantheon, Rome

Interpreting Riegl's writings on architecture, we observe that the "developmen of architecture consisted of an ever complexifying sense of interior space. Beginn with the pyramids, Riegl demonstrated that the path from Egyptian through Gree and Roman to Early Christian architecture could be characterized by both the development and the making symbolic of interior space. The pyramids operated pure, solid forms within the space of the landscape. Their interior chambers, for intents and purposes, were non-existent, for they did not constitute a fundament part of the experience of these structures. The Greek temple, by contrast, while retaining a three dimensional aspect in its siting and its peristyle, contained a sm interior cella which housed a statue of the deity. Although the public did not ent this room, it was able to look into it and interact with it visually. Approaching an proceeding around the building, the experience of the temple was both as a three dimensional form and an interior space. It was an icon itself and the enclosure fo an icon. Like the pyramids, however, both icons remained objects.

Diverging from these precedents, the Pantheon (the example *par excellence* of Roman temple) was confronted not as a freestanding object, but as a two dimensional facade. The emphasis had shifted from the three-dimensional form of the building to the space contained within it. Although housing statues of the deities the space of the Pantheon was itself symbolic. Formed in the shape of a sphere, t experience of the building lay in the reading of its spherical volume as symbolic the geometric perfection of the cosmos. As the knowledge and conceptual framework of man increased, space joined form as a potential bearer of meaning. the structure of knowledge became increasingly conceptual, space became an increasingly important medium of representation. In contrast to the perceptual or e ternal, the conceptual was both grounded in and a projection of the internal "spa of the mind. In this respect, the dome of the Pantheon suggests a rather literal co nection between the form of the cosmos and the form of the human cranium.

Moving from Roman to Early Christian architecture, Riegl presents the Church Sta. Costanza as a developmental transformation of the simple interior volume of the Pantheon. Its domed center space is ringed by an annular vault which extend outward centrifugally through a series of layers. Furthermore, the interior colonn of Sta. Costanza can be read as an inverted peristyle. In this respect it brings to a mination the transformation of the conception of architecture as *form* to the conc tion of architecture as *space*. Form has been turned inside out—space is engaged the primary formal and symbolic medium of architecture.

Reading Riegl's argument according to Hegel's discourse on History (as Riegl's theories are clearly grounded in Hegelian philosophy), one is prompted to align t various stages of architecture to developmental stages of human thought. As suggested above, the development of interior space is analogous to the development conceptual thinking—the development of space parallels the progressive predominance of an ideal (or concept) over/against physical (or perceptual) reality. Truth resides not in the "at hand." It cannot be accessed perceptually, but through a process of abstraction by which perceptual reality is related to an underscoring a overarching ideal. As the mind and the body are differentiated, so is perceptual reality dissociated from whatever perfection it might represent. Man's mind/body dualism is imposed upon the world around him. As the organ of recognition, the

Costanza, Rome. Section showing construction

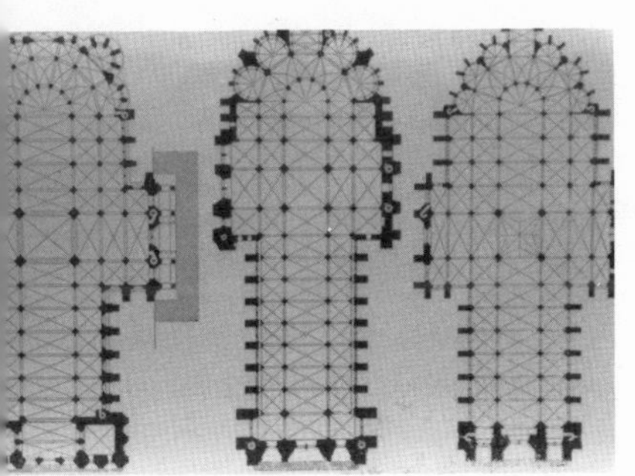

s of Chartres, Reims, and Amiens Cathedrals, century

mind becomes the organ of truth—for it is here that the process of interpretation takes place, and here that the real and ideal worlds are resolved. Within such a mental framework space becomes more effectively symbolic than form. In its essential lack of materiality space is more spiritual, less physically or materially grounded. It is also, as we have noted, symbolically analogous to the space of the mind.

Extrapolating Riegl's argument beyond Early Christian to Gothic architecture (where centric geometries give way to the iconic nave/transept organization of the cathedral), the development of interior space seems to approach a zenith. Accelerating through a proliferation of layers and side aisles, space extends beyond the framework of the exterior walls through large vitrines. It is here that space reaches the limits of its symbolic complexity, moving far beyond the simple spatial volumes of the Roman or Early Christian temple. Following this argument to its analogical conclusion, human thought, too, has now transcended the notions of a simple conceptual ideal. The complexities of Scholastic thought threaten to exhaust the limits of form and figural space, yet remain tenuously confined within the overall iconic program of Christianity. Were this scaffolding to give way, thought would be analogous to a space that refused to conform or be confined to physical and/or geometric parameters. The consequences of this for architecture are obvious—in such a scenario we would confront an utterly dematerialized architecture through which space would freely flow; we would witness the triumph of space over form.

Dealing in just such analogies, the novelist Victor Hugo arrived at similar conclusions half a century before Riegl. Trading back and forth between the conceptual framework of thought and the status of architecture and space, Hugo predicted that thought would abandon architecture as an appropriate and propitious medium. As thought became less and less tied to form, it would increasingly resist representation in architecture. For Hugo the Gothic cathedral represented the limit of the relationship. From the Gothic era onward, the notion of a cohesive conceptual ideal was abandoned in favor of a less corporeal conception of meaning. Meaning now operated fluidly as a set of associations.

In this context, the transmissibility of the printed word was demonstratively more effective than any vessel of stone. No matter how dematerialized, the very stasis of architecture inhibited the flow of meaning. Says Hugo:

Who does not see that in this form [the printed word] *thought is more indelible? Instead of being solid it has become long-lived. It has exchanged durability for immortality. We can demolish a substance, but who can extirpate ubiquity?*

While it is difficult to foresee any future for architecture in these words, it is clear that they bear a more than incidental relationship to Hegelian thought. Like the development of interior space and its deleterious effects on architectural form, the development of human consciousness (once having arrived at clear conceptual categories) is characterized by a progressive "dematerialization" of conceptual ideals. Like architecture opening to the landscape, thought reintegrates with the physical world. It no longer interprets the world on dualistic or symbolic terms, but dynamically and developmentally within the realm of space and time. Accordingly, human nature is in the process of transforming itself from a material to a spiritual state—from form to space and space to spirit. Nor is this transformation effected

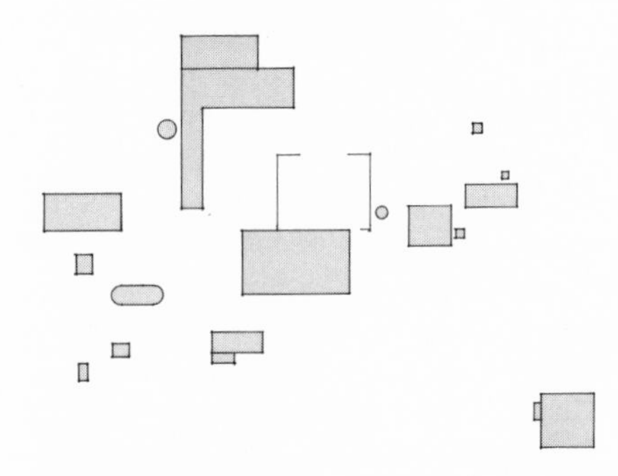

Plan of farm 2. Central Ohio

View, farm 2

transcendentally—each individual through the threshold of death—but within the collective parameters of History.

To a significant extent Hegel and Hugo are allied, although the "Utopian" trajec tory latent in Hegel's discussion of history seems to be conspicuously absent from Hugo. The theories of both writers suggest that form and formal (figural) space hav been rendered obsolete as transmitters of meaning, as meaning is no longer conten to remain within the parameters of a cohesive symbolic agenda. Like meaning, architectural space must be reposited on dynamic terms. In this sense both Hugo anc Hegel anticipate the dematerialized and spatially complex architecture of Modernism. It is also easy to observe, having discussed the Enlightenment in the previou genealogy, the complex interrelationship between political ideology, architectural space, and the philosophical framework. Newton's Absolute Space comes to fruitic in Hugo's dematerialized form; the social Utopian visions of Rousseau and Jefferso flow directly into Hegel's discourse of historical development. The architecture of Modernism, as the inheritor of these ideas, lies somewhere between the discourse dematerialization and that of development (this is the topic of another paper).

And in the context of this argument we may again observe that the American farm compound is proto-modern in its spatial agenda. Conforming to the formal framework of the 18th century and remaining outside of the architecture of the "High Tradition," whose major battles throughout the course of the 19th century were stylistic, the vernacular followed a fairly straightforward course. In so doing, believe that it is through this architecture that the ideals of the Enlightenment are most easily read and flow most easily into the architecture of Modernism.

This statement bears some qualification. By definition the vernacular did not co sciously aspire to the extra-formal and spatially dynamic paradigms suggested by 19th century philosophy. Nor was the "discourse of dematerialization" absent from all other architectures. Certainly this sensibility underscored the "functionally" co ceived iron and glass exhibition structures and train sheds of 19th century Paris ar London. Even the doctrinaire Paris Opera demonstrates a remarkable degree of spa tial complexity when compared with its typological precedents. But an explicit investigation into the status of space remained in the background of architectural co cerns. As an agenda it had yet to be clearly articulated. Similarly, the idea of devel opment, caught up as it was in origins, archeology, and antecedents, could not yet be prospective.

Furthermore, as with Enlightened architecture, the urban context of 19th centur Europe seemed typologically confined within another era. Although Ledoux and other visionaries had managed typological transformations the majority of 19th cer tury urban architecture conformed to the perimeter block/courtyard precedent. In the academic context, from Durand to Gaudet, there was a progressive fragmentation of form along the lines of functional differentiation. But the rules by which these forr were (re)composed remained within the resolved language of classicism.

Largely it was outside of the city and in garden design that radical genealogical speculations were offered. The plan of Walpole's Strawberry Hill, for example, can be read as a loose agglomeration of the garden pavilions that might comprise an 18th century English garden. To this extent it, like much of Gothic Revival architec ture, aspired unconsciously to an asymmetrical and spatially complex paradigm. In so doing it allied its sensibilities with the "low tradition" more than with the high.

Hugo suggests that the return to the language of classicism during the Renaissance represented a regression of sorts, as the Gothic had emerged developmentally from it. Implicit in this suggestion, however, is that architecture had no choice—in a structural sense, the materials of Gothic architecture had reached the limits of their compressive capabilities and would support no further dematerialization (the classical revivals from the Renaissance onward represented a kind of biding-of-time until technology advanced to coincide with the spatial and material aspirations of architecture); in an ideological sense, form was a regressive concept. When scrutinized rationally, however, the Gothic held some promise as a revival style. Its latent structural rationalism suggested an architecture conceived outside of the parameters of a symbolic program and prefigured a transformation from the symbolic to the dynamically functional. The concept of a dynamic architecture and the concept of function came together in the question of "how," (method) as "what" (symbolic reference or meaning) had been the operative question in an architecture of representation (classical architecture). It was not a question of trading one symbolic paradigm for another, for to represent dynamism would be to remain within the essentially static program of representation. The question itself had to be reformulated. In the absence of a paradigm, it became, as with science, a question of method.

In Hugo's argument, the low tradition (within which he enshrines the Gothic cathedral) has always been in the possession of "the people." In its demotic underpinnings it has existed in counterposition to the hierarchical and highly formalized architecture of absolute government—whether that of Imperial Rome or the France of the Bourbons. To reject absolute government (which operates by clearly locating the nexus of power) or formalized religion and philosophy (which locate power in a conceptually displaced Monad) is to reject absolute power. It is to seize upon a system of thinking and a language of architecture which remain anachronistic and relative. It is to diffuse power among a number of individuals; it is to compose form in such a way that the part is not dominated by the whole; it is to disperse meaning among the "sum total" of interpretations—restricting questions of value to issues of efficacy and distinguishing such questions from the concept of Truth. For Hugo, the demotic tradition (the Gothic/vernacular) posed a challenge to symbolism and its repressive implications. By its very definition, the possibility of a transcendent "what" or object of symbolic reference removed power from the possession of the people. Symbolism bespoke an "other" which operated over/against self; it was the usurping of individual responsibility to serve the ends of collective interpretation.

A similar design to "liberate" meaning operated in the exhortations of Ruskin who sought to rescue meaning from the manipulative processes of industrial production. Like Hugo, he advocated architecture as a process in which an explicit formal agenda would be sacrificed at the hands of the craftsman.

Like the image of the Gothic offered by Hugo and Ruskin, American architecture falls within the demotic tradition—politically democratic and unconsciously referencing the fragmentation of precedents such as the architecture of pre-Hellenistic Greece. It is an architecture of, for, and by the people in which the aspirations of the collective support the aspirations of the individual, in which the polysemic and

View, farm 6

View, farm 5

decentralization are enshrined. But to confine it within a tradition would be to paralyze it, for the term "tradition" carries no developmental implications. As a tradition, the demotic (vernacular) would be assigned a complementary rather than adversarial position relative to formalized architecture. Within the developmental discourse of Hugo and Hegel, however, the fragmentation of American architecture can be read as symptomatic. It is not simply the persistence of an architectural undercurrent but a decisive manifestation of the overcoming of the hieratic by the demotic—its fragmentation is the inheritor of the Gothic. In its rationalized randomness it belies an epistemological shift—the superceding of a formal (conceptual) framework by a notion of functional self-evidency—a shift from the "what" of reference to the "how" of method. In the absence of an absolute nexus of power, be it divine or governmental, there remains no conceptual framework in which to conceive a unified architecture. Having abandoned the formal framework of the previous eras, questions of form can no longer be posed referentially. Turning to function, architecture attempts to assume whatever form is most propitious to its function: accreting as would any natural substance. Here the reference remains internal form to function. The operative question, as in all aspects of nature and scientific inquiry during the 19th century, was no longer one of representation. It made no sense, for instance, to ask what a dog meant or stood for, so why should architectu be subjected to such an inquiry?

It is important to distinguish this notion of functional reference from its counterpart in the theoretical architecture of the 18th century. As in Ledoux's wood cutter house, which assumed the form of a pile of logs, allusions to function remained essentially symbolic. By contrast, the functionalism of the vernacular was neither symbolic nor self-conscious. While the forms themselves belie certain stylistic predispositions, the arrangement of those forms bespeaks a veritable inability to operate (conceptualize) formally. As with scientific inquiry, questions of formal arrangement appear irrelevant apart from the question of function. The very form of the question ha changed. Formal arrangement has been marginalized as a concern—akin to pattern and decoration. The concept of style is itself a product of this marginalization.

The very lack of reference in the forms of the farmstead underscores their abstract quality. In the seeming self-evidency of their aspect and position, no questio are asked. Rather, it is silence we encounter when interacting with these forms, a silence which is somehow deafening given the intention which seems latent in the specificity of their placement. We uncover a series of incidental decisions underscored by peculiar presumptions about expediency. Here the grid is an organizatioal red herring. How and why these compositions appear to operate as compositions has little to do with intention. And it is precisely this lack of intention which separates this architecture both from the "high tradition" (specifically the language of classicism) and from the architecture of Modernism in which similar compositiona tendencies are posited within an ideological agenda. In the absence of intention the rural vernacular is neither symbolic nor paradigmatic of a revision in the direction of aspiration. It refers to nothing beyond itself nor is it conscious of itself as such.

While the farmstead is the clearest example of conceptual and architectural fragmentation within American architecture, such fragmentation is evidenced in the traditionally anachronistic relationships between buildings within American urban

sition of forms, farm 5

grids. Since Jefferson isolated the Maison Caree within the open landscape of Richmond, Virginia, there has been a tradition of classical and/or Beaux Arts implants in America which remain isolated and/or uncoordinated with their urban environments. Given the axial proclivities of the classical language, the disconnection of these buildings seems especially symptomatic. If not for the farm we would interpret these phenomena differently.

Moreover, working from the vernacular, indigenous "high" American architecture such as the Shingle style set the stage for the further breakdown of interior space. Like Strawberry Hill, Shingle style houses are often agglomerations of apparently discrete forms. In plan, however, the potential figurality of these volumes is compromised through large scale openings which allow space to flow freely from one volume to another. While American buildings operate "objectively" in their relationship to the landscape, space is never conceived on such terms. Both without and within space tends toward the atopic.

GENEALOGY #3: THE MODERN MOVEMENT

While underscoring the architectural theories of 19th century Europe, the discourse of development blossomed in the ideology of the avant-garde. Remaining within the framework of history, the avant-garde shifted its trajectory from the past to the future. It was no longer a question of recovering Arcadia, but of achieving Utopia.

In the discourse of development, the dynamic overcomes the static. Pre-existent architectural language, like governmental authority, was considered to have operated within a conceptual framework which, in its recalcitrance, impeded the dynamic transformation of society. The avant-garde sought not only a language appropriate to this dynamic paradigm, but one that was grounded in the sensibilities of the common man. As with Hugo, the dynamic and the popular went hand in hand; the revolution, whether in industry, government, or the arts, was a popular revolution.

In the context of populism it is easy to speculate on how the vernacular might have functioned as a paradigm for the avant-garde. Not only did its formal and spatial proclivities lie outside of the traditional discourse of formal resolution, but it was also historically aligned with the common man.

The elision of the notion of progress with the image of popular culture brought together two disparate elements and set the stage for a formal predisposition (however unconscious) toward the vernacular. While it is difficult and perhaps unnecessary to pinpoint a direct influence of the vernacular on the European avant-garde, indirect influences abound. As concerns American vernacular, Marinetti was an avid reader of Walt Whitman—from whom he acquired both the taste for technology and his love for the common man. It was perhaps Whitman's romanticism of progress which allowed Marinetti to mistake the victim of industrialization for its champion, and to ally the idea of progress with the cause of the common man. Writes Marinetti:

You may have noticed in the last great railway strike in France that the Sabotage committees could not persuade a single mechanic to put his locomotive out of action.…I find this natural enough. How could a man kill so faithful and devoted a friend?

K. Malevich, *The Floor Polishers* 1911

Outbuildings. Shakertown, Kentucky

Marc Chagall, *The Dead Man* 1908

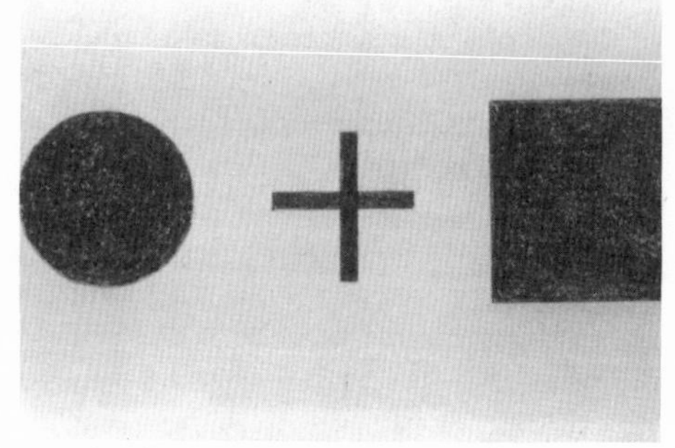

K. Malevich, *Contrasting Suprematist Elements* c. 1915

K. Malevich, *Red Square and Black Square* c. 19

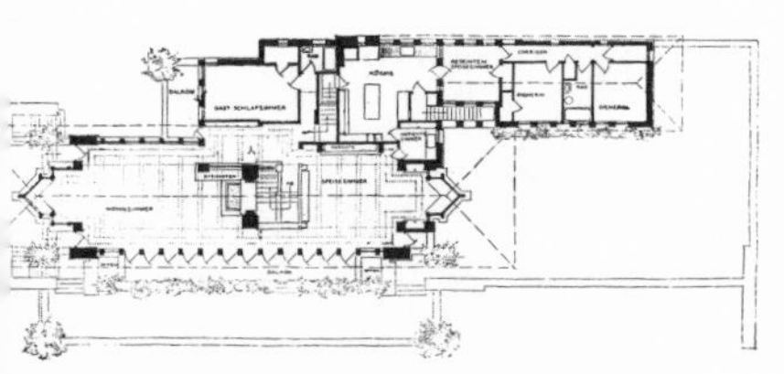

Wright, Robie House. Chicago, Illinois 1906

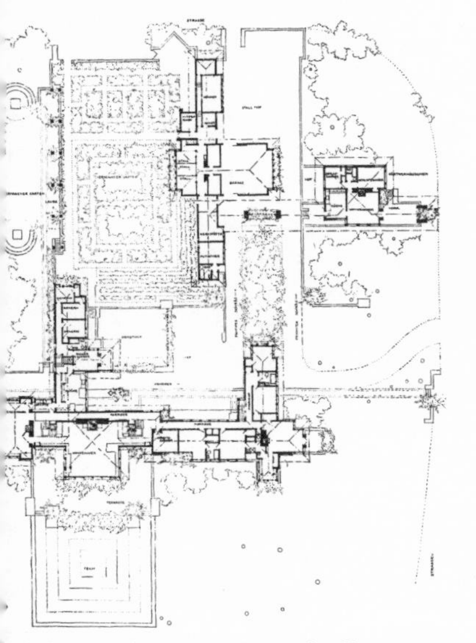

Wright, Coonley House. Riverside, Illinois 1908

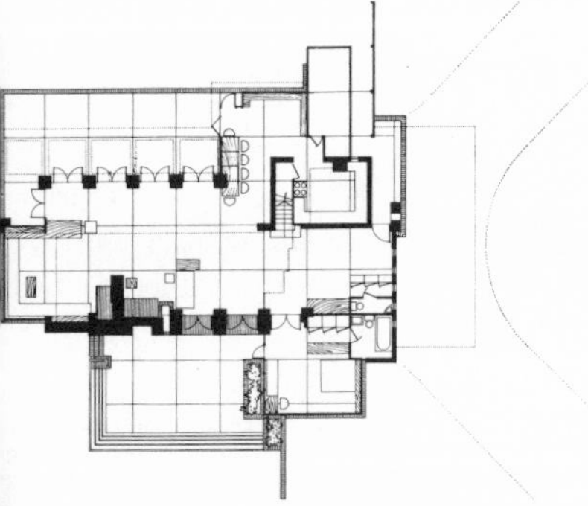

Wright, Schwartz House. Two Rivers, onsin 1939

The work of the constructivists, despite cubism's influence upon it, sought an aesthetic "lowest common denominator" from which to begin the process of building. Not surprising, then, were the forays of the proponents of constructivism (Malevich, El Lissitzky) into the Jewish ghettos of the Pale to search for inspiration among vernacular art and handicraft. As with the futurists, they believed that a popular revolution was best grounded in the sensibilities of the people.

While constructivist art swerved away from the literal folk references characteristic of the art of Chagall, it belies an understanding of the iconic basis of Russian art. In this respect the suprematist work of Malevich can be read as a new iconic language in which specific references have been eliminated to anticipate the values that might replace them. His suprematist works are "open-ended icons" waiting to absorb the values of a reformed society. While their folk appeal is not as literal as Chagall's imagery, the abstracted and basic quality of Malevich's geometric forms is meant to be universal. And certainly the application of constructivist graphics to such familiar items as dishware indicates a desire to ground the aesthetic in the discourse of the everyday.

For its myriad influences and agendas, the avant-garde arrived at a formal language not at all dissimilar to the operative language of American vernacular. Inversely, while the buildings of the farmsteads remain within the orthogonality of the American grid, their elemental forms and dynamic compositions seem Supremetist in inspiration. A similar sensibility is operative in both. Continuing this analogy, the moralistic overtones of Loos's essay on ornament seem "puritanical" to such an extent that the uninitiated might not distinguish between his white stucco boxes and the stripped down dwellings of the Shakers. And when Berlage evokes the "natural" as the paradigm for architecture in its ability to achieve "unity in plurality," he anticipates an architecture which operates outside of the artificial geometries of classicism—in which the individuality of the parts is not subsumed by the larger composition, and in which the parts are grouped to form a dynamic balance. When he writes that "in architecture, decoration and ornament are quite inessential while space creation and the relationship of masses are its true essentials," one imagines an arrangement of elemental masses which inadvertently recalls the farm grouping.

More literal connections between the American vernacular and the forms of the avant-garde can be made through the work of Frank Lloyd Wright. Having come across the second edition of the Wasmuth portfolio in 1911, Berlage was instrumental in introducing the work of Wright to Rietveld and to his students, including Mies van der Rohe. Even before the formulation of the De Stijl group in 1916, one of its members, Robert van t'Hoff, had been to Chicago to see Wright's work. The influence of Wright on that group can be seen as early as 1916 in van t'Hoff's villa at Huis ter Heide and is still very much present in Rietveld's Shroeder House of 1925.

While the historical connection between Wright and the avant-garde is undeniable, it becomes relevant to this argument only to the extent that Wright's work can be shown to be grounded in the sensibilities of the American vernacular. Given his childhood in rural Wisconsin, I believe that suggestion is not only reasonable but can be demonstrated in several significant ways. First, like the farm compound, Wright's work evidences the tendency to individuate functional parts: living, dining, entry, service. While initially these four components were arranged (however dis-

Theo van Doesburgh, *Composition XXII* 1920

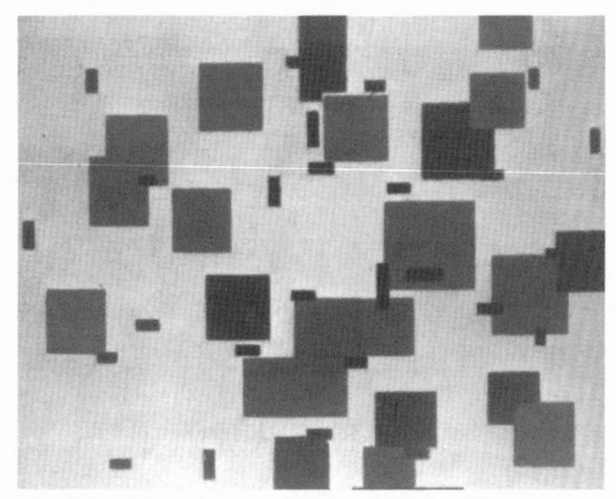
Piet Mondrian, *Composition with Color Planes on White Ground* 1917

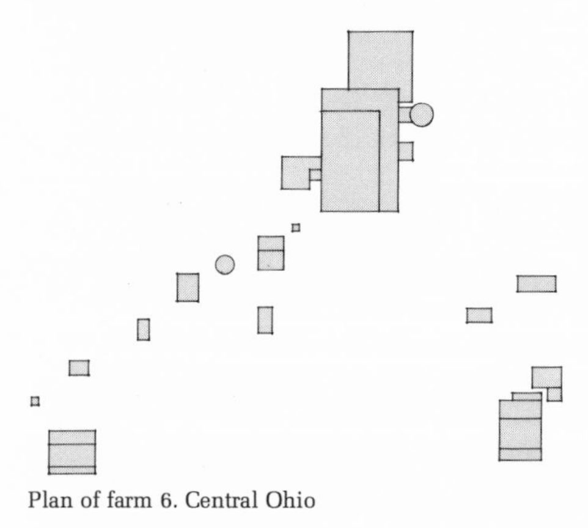
Plan of farm 6. Central Ohio

cretely) within the confines of a box, in his houses of the early part of this centur the components are articulated separately.

Secondly, having been formally differentiated, the functional components are composed in a pinwheel configuration, usually arranged around a solid, central el ment or hearth. In such arrangements alignments are not made axially (center to c ter) but in relationships of center to edge or right to left edge. Accordingly, one moves through the system diagonally, from one volume to the next.

Both the pinwheel configuration and the diagonal path of movement are chara teristic of the farm compound, where the four corners of the farmyard (as defined component buildings) are left open, and movement is pushed to the edges. The same center-to-edge alignments occur. Within the context of an open landscape th arrangement is more appropriate than the traditionally frontal courtyard type. Wh Wright's earlier houses retain a strong sense of frontality, later prototypes, such as the Suntop Houses and the components of Broadacre City, abandon all such frontality. In these examples, as with the prototypical farm and town, there is an impl cit and equal connection to adjacent structures in all four directions.

Thirdly, while the pinwheel dynamically activates the composition of Wright's houses, the pieces remain in an orthogonal relationship to each other—as if affixe within an invisible grid. Like the orthogonal relationships which predominate within the farm and town, this grid can be understood as a subset of the municipa grid, which, in turn, is a subset of the continental grid. Via the grid, the orthogonality of the house evokes space and connections at an extremely broad scale.

This reference to the landscape in Wright's work is made not only abstractly, b literally, by pushing the volumes to the perimeter of the composition and opening them up with glass. As with the farm, the focus is predominantly outward, toward the landscape. No internalized spatial focus is made.

While the plan configuration strategies of Wright's houses can be related to the farm, differences abound. The material aspect of the houses departs from the skel tal prototype of the farm buildings. In so doing, they also depart from another pro type available to Wright, namely the Shingle style houses being built by McKim, Mead and White. This is significant in that the plan configurations of these house also favor the pinwheel. In so doing they allude to similar rural vernacular source

More importantly, the horizontal aspiration of Wright's forms represents a radic departure from the vertical punctuation of the farm forms. While formally more dynamic, they are geometrically less pure. But because it is in the integrity and abstraction of its volumes that the farm compound most closely resembles de Stijl compositions, we might suggest that de Stijl received mediated information from Wright which it re-abstracted back to its sources. Comprised as it is of volumetric rather than planar components, the purity of its volumes and the planarity of its s faces allow the farm compound to operate in a manner similar to the planar compositions of De Stijl. And in plan the orthogonal composition of the farmstead is v tually identical to the colored rectangles within the compositions of Van Doesburg and Mondrian. Both are composed of "random" rectilinear elements, both are organized within a grid.

As with the previous genealogy, this argument is not one of causality but of com mon parentage. Like the spatial proclivities of the American vernacular, the "Unive

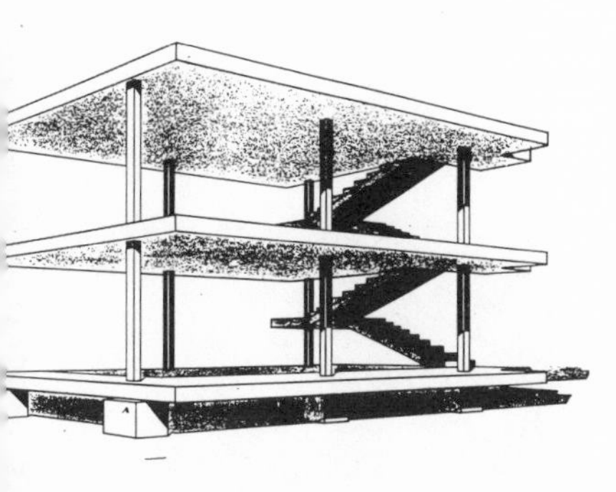

;orbusier, Diagram of Maison Domino, 1914

ical frame and skin structure, American barn

ı, farm 5

sal" spatial program of de Stijl was grounded both in the Absolute Space of the Enlightenment and in the subsequent discourse of dematerialization. In this respect, points of tangency between the two architectures represent moments of self-recognition more than conscious or causal influence.

Moving to the architecture of Le Corbusier we uncover additional alignments. Certainly Le Corbusier was an ideological proponent of the vernacular and quoted freely from provincial French sources in several of his houses (Maisons Jaoul). But it is in the structural system of the Maison Domino that significant relationships are suggested between his architecture and the architecture of the American farm.

The history of European architecture is to a great extent the history of masonry architecture. Especially in residential construction, the bearing wall predominated. Deletions of surface necessitated the addition of piers and buttressing as the facade supported not only itself, but the floor joists as well. With the Maison Domino system Le Corbusier revolutionized the facade. By employing a system of columns internal to the volume of the building, he separated the building's structure from its facade. This enabled him to use lighter, non-loadbearing materials for the surface of the building and to position openings within that surface in innovative ways. Freed of the exigencies of weight, the proportion of openings could also change.

More radically, since the "facade" was holding nothing up, the facade itself could be lifted from the ground. The base, traditionally the most massive portion of the building, could now be eliminated—allowing the groundplane to run continuously beneath it. We see this dematerialization in a number of his villas.

While representing a radical departure from the structural traditions of European architecture, the Maison Domino system closely resembles frame and siding construction. As such, the structural and elevational innovations arrived at by le Corbusier had enjoyed a long tradition in American wood-frame building. His taut, white gunite surfaces had an analogue in the whitewashed siding of American architecture. Within both systems the facade acts as a sort of "curtain wall" stretched over (rather than supporting) the structural frame of the building.

The similarity in structure and surface combined with an apparently functional compositional strategy, results in surprising similarities between the residential work of le Corbusier and the elevations of typical American farm outbuildings. As with the villas of Le Corbusier, openings in these buildings appear random, according to the functional exigency of a given position. And because neither bears nor supports weight, the skins of both buildings could be cut away in substantial ways. Thus the similarity is heightened by a common relationship to the groundplane: farm buildings are often lifted off the ground to discourage vermin and moisture penetration. A tractor parked beneath a corn crib inadvertently recalls the "airplane fuselage" tucked beneath Maison Cook or the automobiles huddled under the wings of the Villa Savoie. The simple geometries of the forms also prefigure the white boxes of Le Corbusier; both stand isolated and absolute within their landscapes. Furthermore, the directionality of their gables along with their apparent disconnection from the groundplane lends them the animated quality of the Maison Citrohan. While at home in the landscape, they are mobile and belong to no place in particular.

Finally there is a similar attitude about mass production and obsolescence present in both the farm and the work of Le Corbusier. Made as it is of wood and

Barn, farm 2

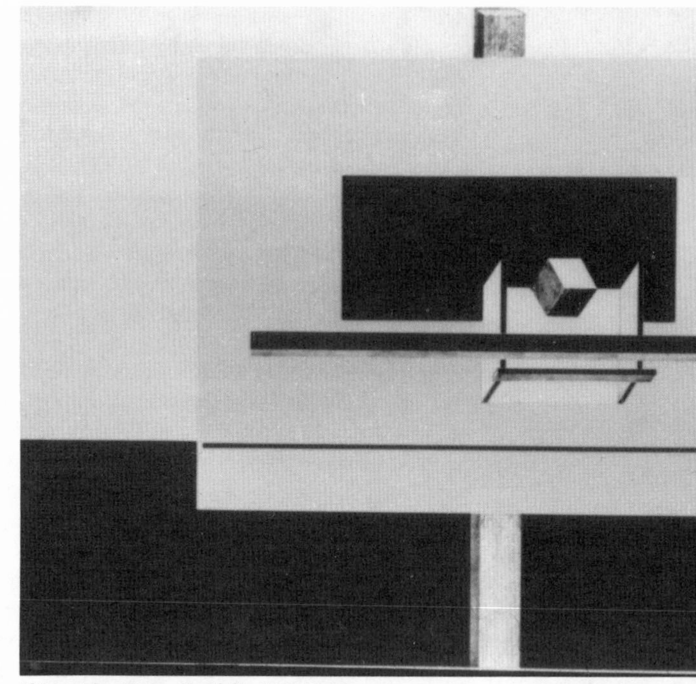
El Lissitzky, *Proun Portfolio #3* 1919–23

Le Corbusier, Les Terraces, Garches. Seine-et-Oise 1927–28

Barn, farm 1

Le Corbusier, Cook House, Paris. 1926

shrouded with a perforated skin, the lifespan of the outbuilding seems tentative. According to utility, one may be replaced by another, or, as is more often the case, another will be built adjacent to it. This consequential repetition of similar forms further breaks down the unique relation of form to place. Identical forms appear at various places at once recalling a graveyard of mass-produced objects set out to pasture. While this observation is more intuitive than analytical, a common sensibility seems to pervade both architectures.

ted structure. Newark, Ohio

ing and trailer, farm 2

CONCLUSION

In the course of this essay I have attempted to set forth several genealogies that reveal and elaborate the apparently coincidental relationship of the American rural vernacular to Modern architecture. This explains, in part, the successful implantation of European Modernism on American soils. Not only did the immigration of European educators to America hasten the acceptance of the Modernist agenda, but the spatial proclivities of this country set the stage for its arrival.

As noted, the argument is not one of causal influence but of epistemological tangency. Both architectures participate in the shift which becomes manifest in 18th century thought and formalized in the developmental discourse of dematerialization. This strain remains latent in American architecture while becoming explicit in the ideology of the avant-garde. The two architectures converge at certain points through such figures as Frank Lloyd Wright, but to a great extent their similarity remains as coincidental as it is inevitable.

The value of this exegesis is not so much in its ability to recognize potential similarities between disparate objects as it is to suggest new ways to evaluate both the American city and American vernacular. Due to its lack of conformity to "acceptable" urban principles, the former is often misunderstood—the symptoms are mistaken for problems. As concerns the vernacular, more often than not it is overlooked as being irrelevant to or marginal within the discourse of architecture. Perhaps its very exclusion bespeaks a repressed sense of its relevancy.

Our initial comparison of the city to the farmstead suggests that different prototypes are operative within the city than we might imagine or prescribe. Likewise, the comparison of the farmstead to the architecture of Modernism suggests that there are more comprehensive ways of dealing with the architecture at hand and that Modernism in America did not represent a break with the past (as was the case in European society) but was well within the "tradition" of the way we view ourselves and our landscape. As such, the politics of Modernism do not suggest that we abandon our proclivities in favor of European imports (including the discourse of the 19th century city so popular in post-modern discourse), but investigate our architecture on its own terms and so discover the existing alignments.

I acknowledge that these alignments have been suggested by such historians as Vincent Scully, who evaluated the architecture of American Modernists (Gwathmey, Venturi, Meier) against the indigenous architecture of the Shingle style. But to strengthen these art-historical arguments with a strong theoretical base is to reintroduce the possibility of an architecture which, although fundamentally Modern, retains a strong cultural resonance.

van Shiles

Some Words about the Ohio Landscape

Central Ohio, in a condensed view, is a flat plain marked by a regular, orthogonal grid of state highways, local routes, and farm roads. This plain and grid, along with the horizon, form the context for the farm compounds that are the subjects of this catalogue. The grid organizes the ground and forms a large scale parcelization and infrastructure for the compounds. Since the initial experience of this landscape is from the car, the grid remains a primary point of reference: a visitor to a farm marks his position in the landscape relative to the road which brought him there.

Seen from the highway, the farm compounds are a collection of buildings[1] that give a clear sense of precinct framed by the horizon and roads. Here the compound has a figural presence in the landscape. The collection of volumes read against the horizon and plain and in relation to another complex, perhaps a mile away, has an object-like quality. From outside the compound the buildings are striking white objects of volumetric clarity resting on the ground. The shadows cast by the buildings make a connection between the light, white objects and the solid ground.

Moving into the compound, now walking away from the road, these white volumes begin to frame the landscape. The ground plain and the horizon are captured by the edges of the volumes. From inside, the compound is a group of buildings which suggest an urban condition of autonomous buildings gathered together to make a space and delimit the landscape while simultaneously allowing the space to run to the horizon. From the interior of the complex it is the individual buildings which have the figural presence. The buildings are simple volumes with complex surfaces. The white skins are pulled tight and have little relief except for the slight cave and its shadow. Openings which when shut complete the tight volume, may slide, hinge, or be tethered. Glazed punctures in the skin begin to reveal the depth of the outermost surface.

As you move into the building the nature of the construction and the layering of surfaces belies the previous reading of them as pure volumes. The buildings now reveal themselves as thin-skinned containers with a light side and a dark side. The thin outer layer of white is supported by the darkness of the interior, and it is the object which this container houses, animal or machine, that is figural. The openings now frame building fragments and pieces of the horizon. From inside the building the fragility of the white surface is revealed and the initial reading of these volumes in the landscape is altered. The movement from outside the compound to inside the building reflects the shifting set of relationships between structure and landscape and the changing perception of figure to context.

The pieces documented in this catalogue are sponsored by these observations.

1. These are generic, authorless buildings; we've seen them before.

IMAGES FROM THE EXHIBITION
Benjamin Gianni

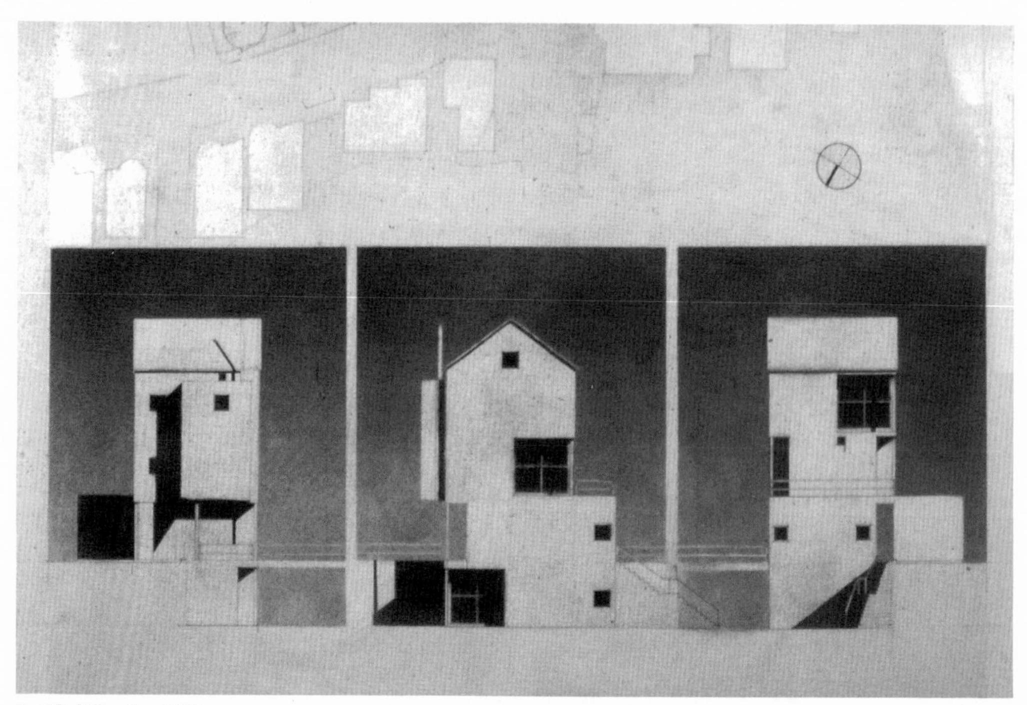

Untitled Housing 1987

Dice Thrown, 1987

Modern Times 1, 1988

Friday @ 3:00 pm, 1988

ern Times 2, 1988

High Noon, 1987

Farm Fiction 1, 1988

Farm Fiction 2, 1988

n Fiction 3, 1988

Ohio Houses, 1987

ɔect #9, 1987

Morphology, 1987

Hindsight : 9, 1987

Farm Fiction Prospect, 1988

pect #8, 1987

IMAGES FROM THE EXHIBITION
Bryan Shiles

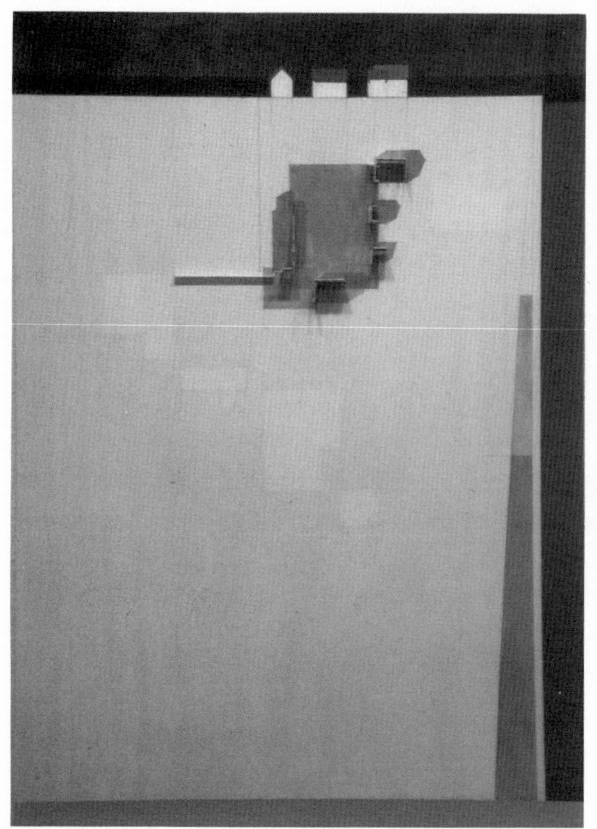

Construction 2

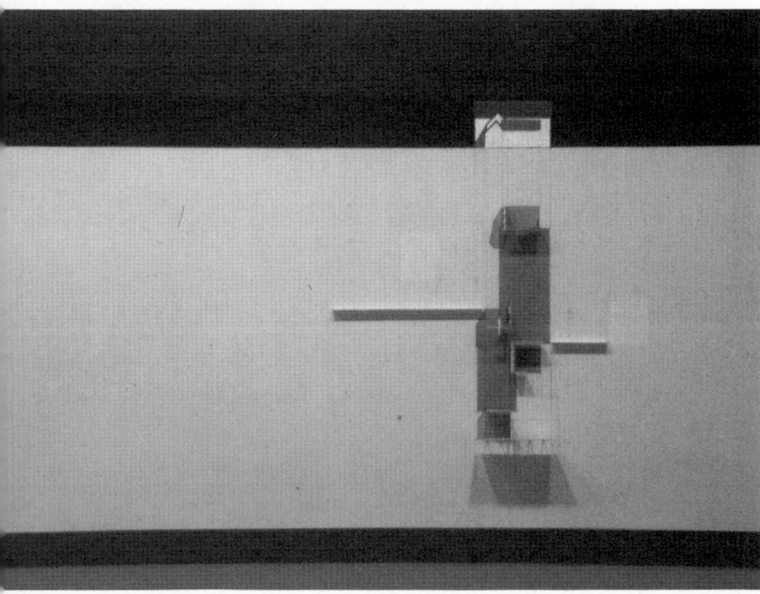

truction 5

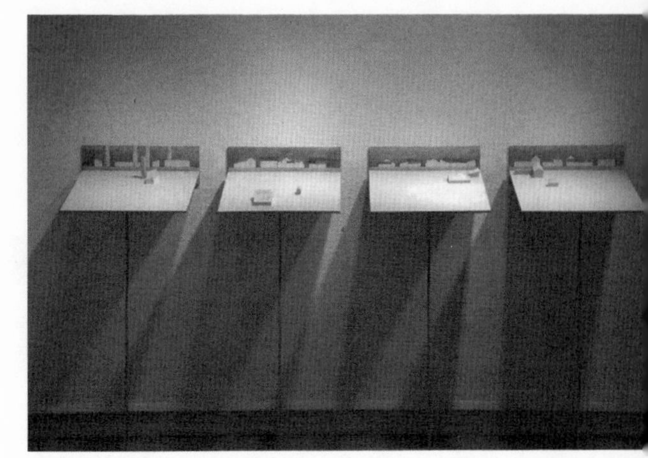
Platform 1–4

In/Out Tool 1, 1988

n's Rib *(B. Gianni)*

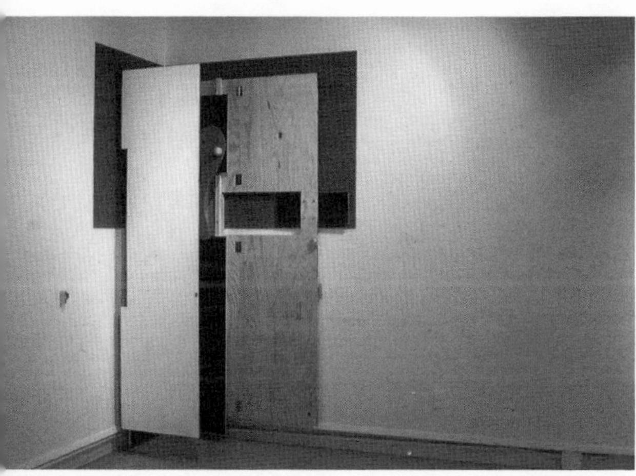
ıt Tool 2, 1988

In/Out Tool 3, 1988

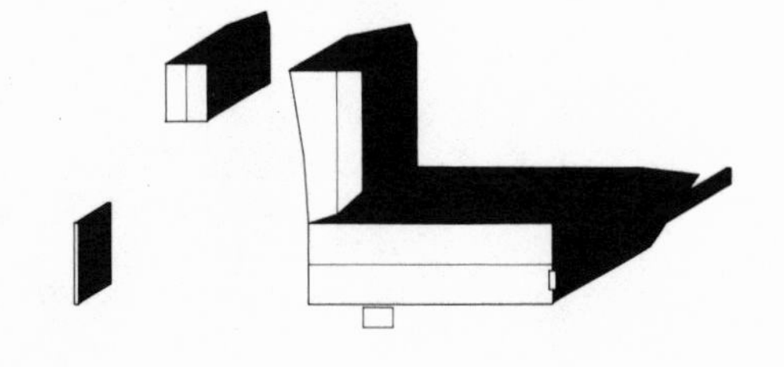

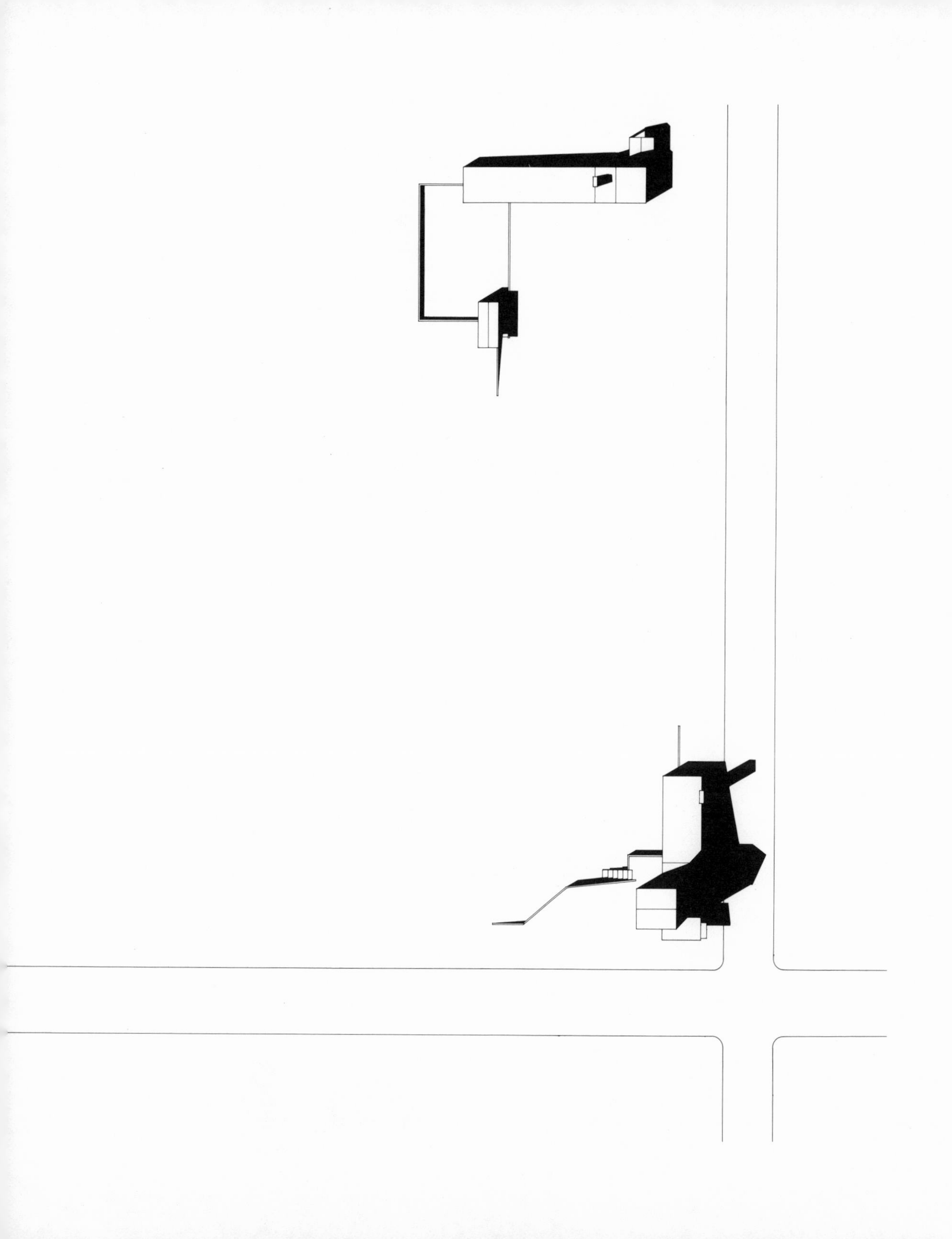

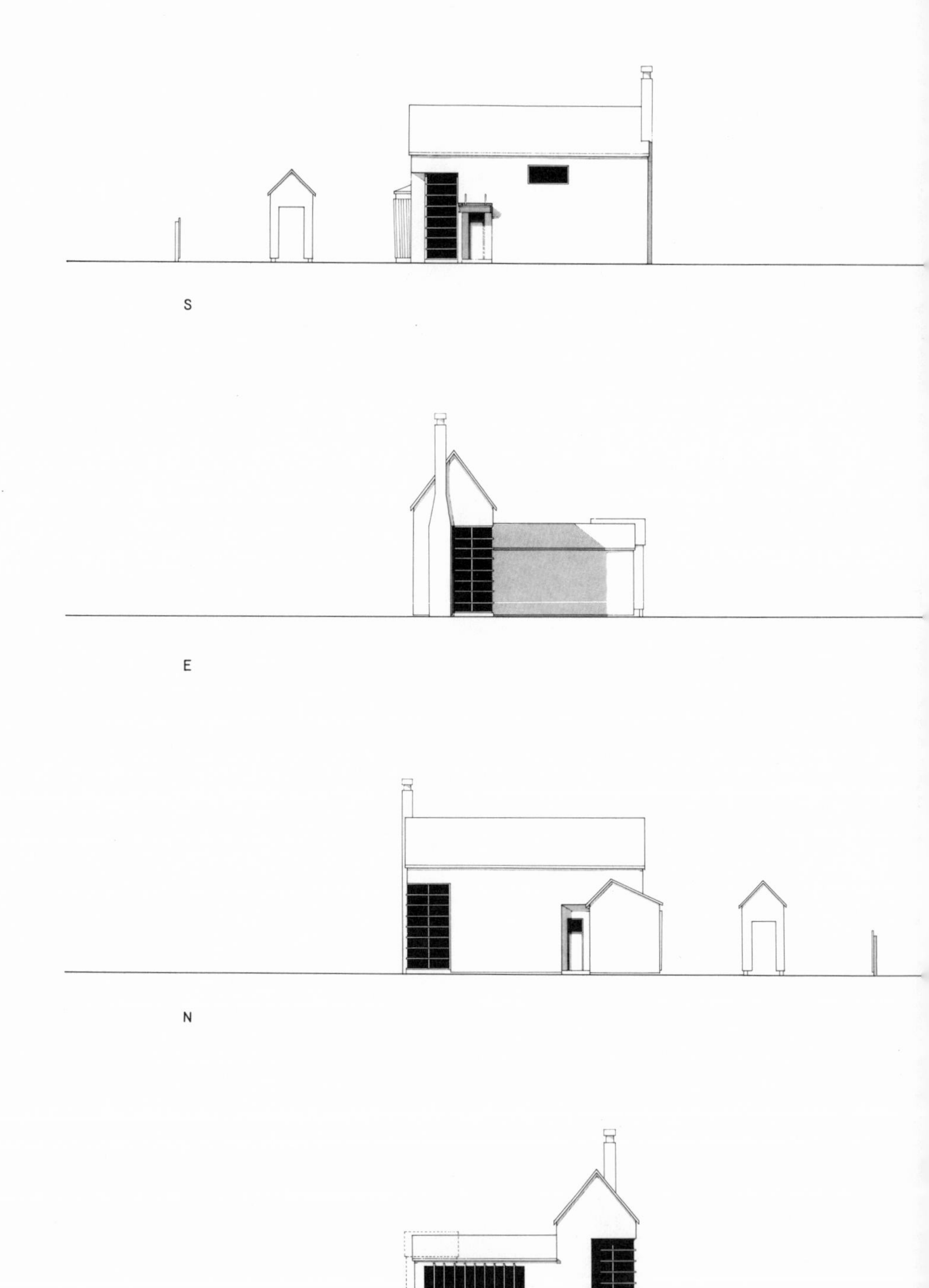
S
E
N

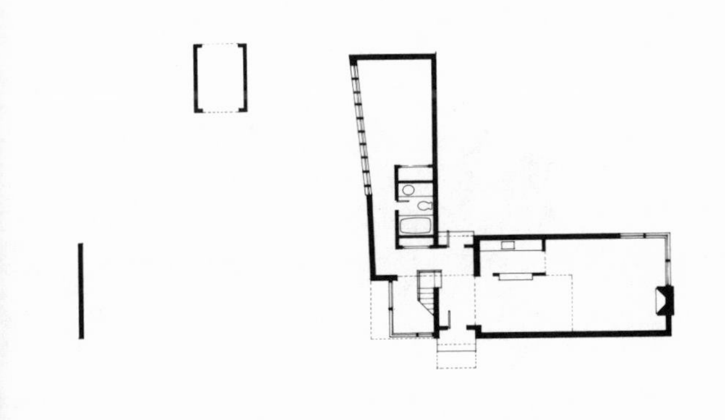

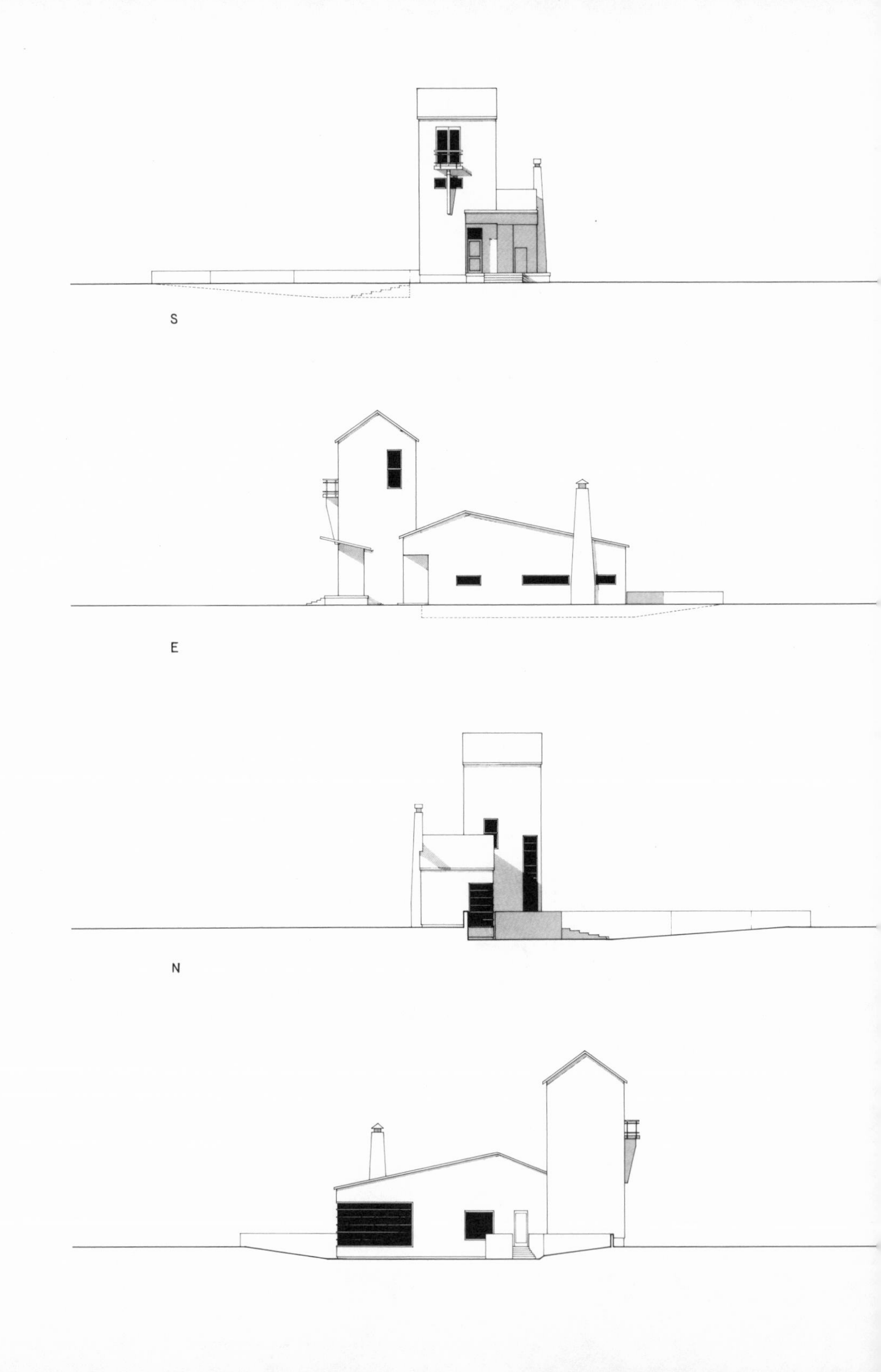
S
E
N

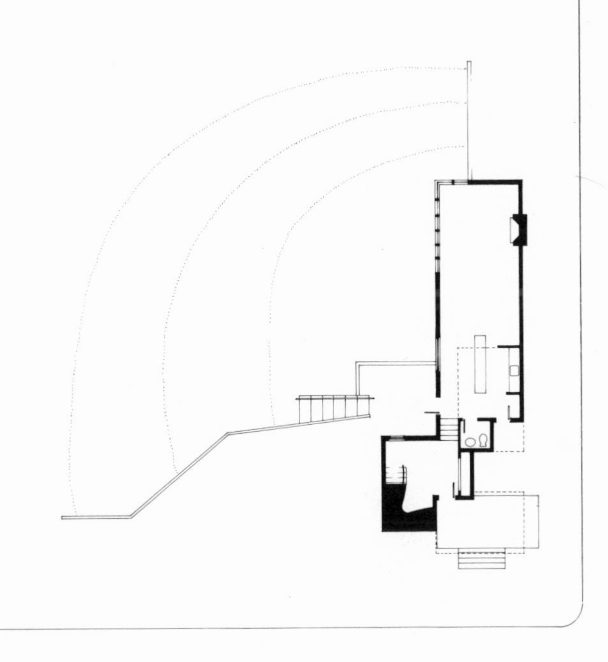

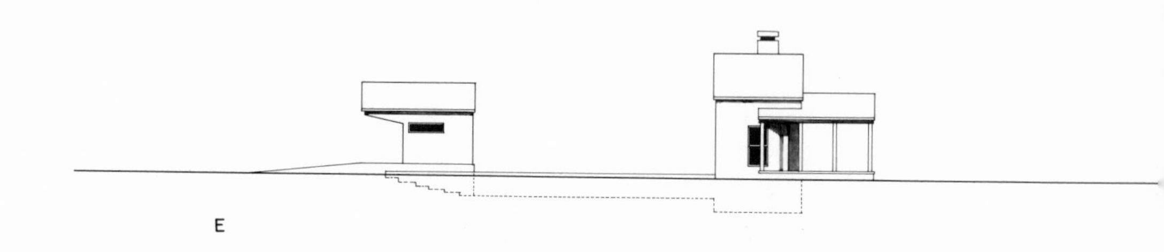

E

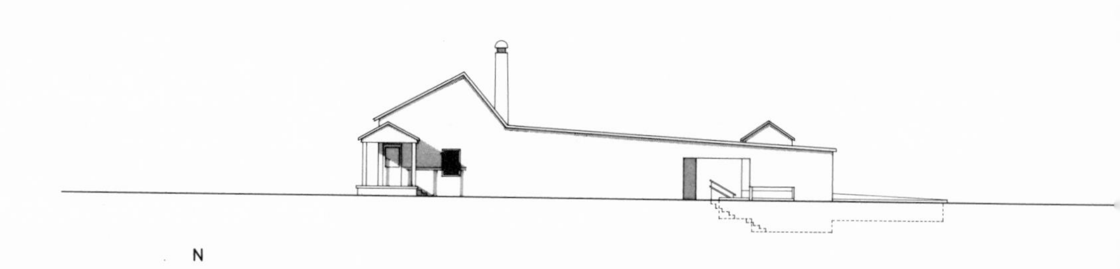

N

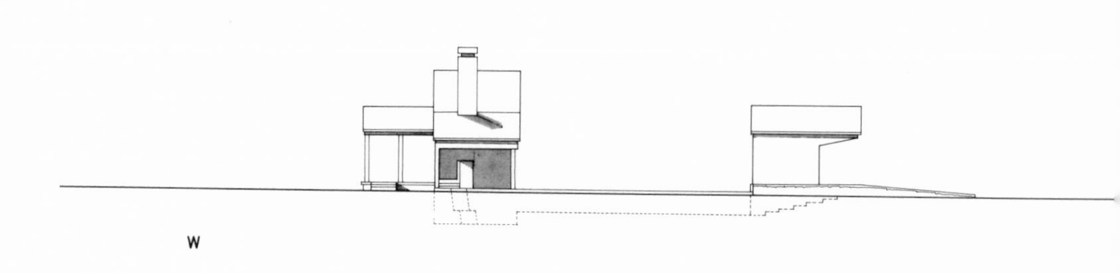

W

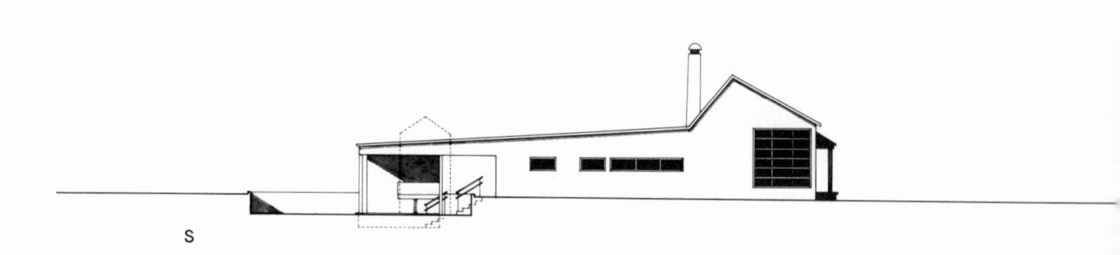

S

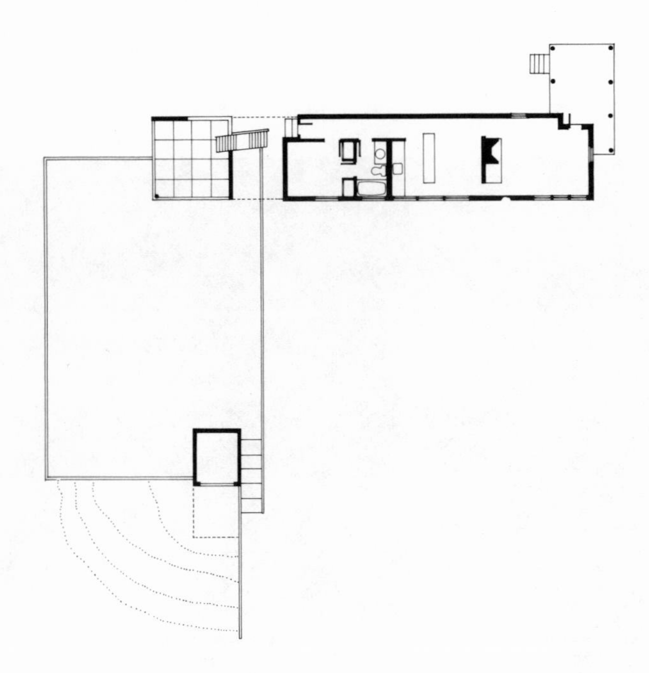

IMAGES FROM THE EXHIBITION

Kevin Kemner

Decompositions 1: Bank Barn

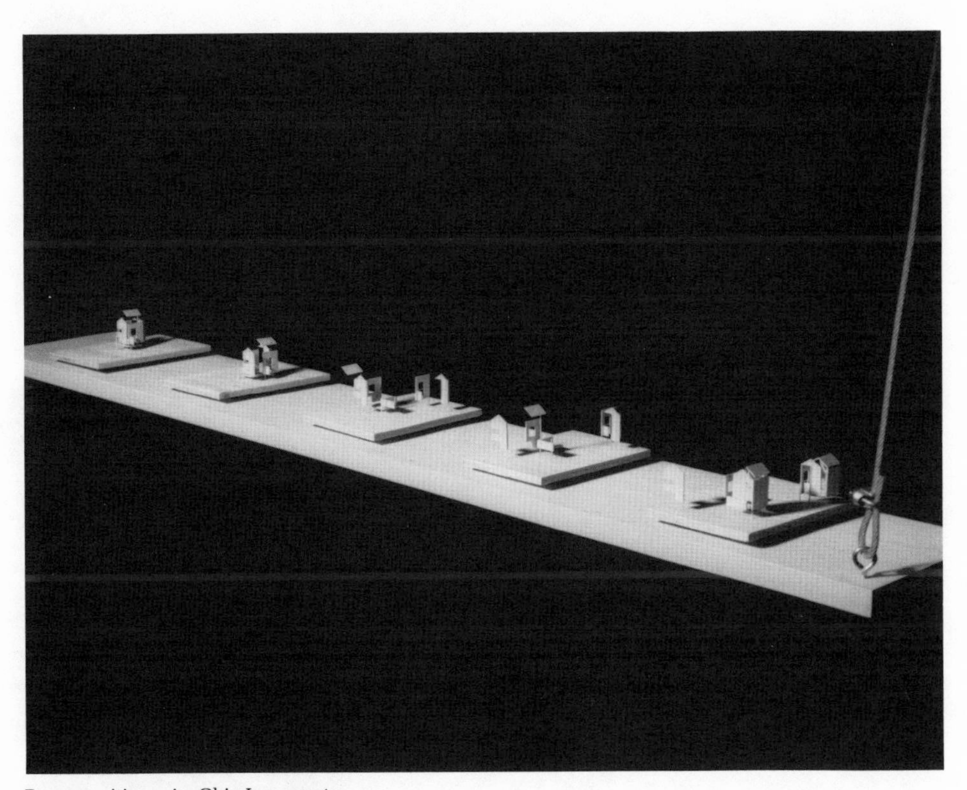

Recompositions: An Ohio Impromptu

Decomposition 1: Bank Barn

Decomposition 3: Monitors

mposition 3: Monitors

omposition 1: Bank Barn

Strategies (upper) *(K. Kemner, B. Gianni)*

Strategies (lower) *(K. Kemner, B. Gianni)*

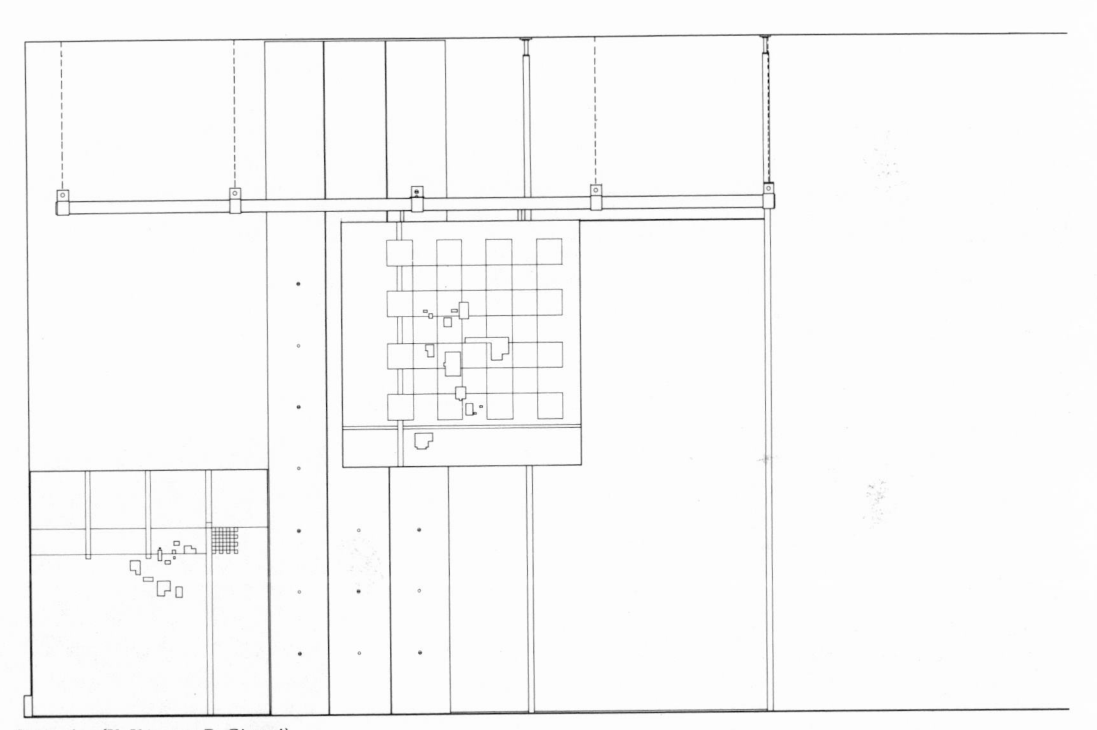

Strategies *(K. Kemner, B. Gianni)*

pose, an answer, a question

spokesmen

Speakers

Barns, marking the dance place w/o distinctions

Proximity

In each pose an answer

Jonah: In the eye of Leviathan

An architecture

mute sirens dancing

intentions Arbitrary

Vernacular arbitrary

Dancers Pose

Answer by Arrangement. Caught

Answer by Question

finding what is sought

clusters of Dancers

Each an arrangement.

Alibi

Markers –

an answer

by pose

Precarious.

upon the precarious field of answers

Answers upon the

Caught of position

seeking

Questioning

The abandonment of an arbitrary surface

Recievers of questions

Notating answers, barns

Marking a reply

presenting pose upon

Markers

Barns posing

maintained by proximity

An Answer seeking validity

Caught between positions

A pose questioned

Barns receiving questions?

Scattered upon the landscape, silent sirens dance temptation, promising to reveal private intentions. Caught between positions, abandoned to an arbitrary surface, a dance maintained by proximity. Arrangement. A reply of position, barns pose, revelations on an uncertain field.

ISBN 0-910413-62-2